MANAGEMENT AUDITING

MANAGEMENT AUDITING

A Questionnaire Approach

Robert J. Thierauf

A DIVISION OF AMERICAN MANAGEMENT ASSOCIATIONS

Library of Congress Cataloging in Publication Data

Thierauf, Robert J
  Management auditing.

  Bibliography: p.
  Includes index.
  1. Management audit. I. Title.
HD58.95.T48   658.1'51   79-21766
ISBN 0-8144-5535-2

First Printing

Dedicated
to the memory of
D. J. O'Conor, Sr.,
a co-founder of the
Formica Corporation

Preface

DESPITE IMPORTANT ADVANCES in management principles and practices, little has been published on management auditing, that is, the essentials of management audits or how to go about conducting one. Briefly, management audits are what their name implies: audits of management. They appraise the *quality* of managers, or, more precisely, their ability to accomplish specific objectives as well as assigned tasks.

In view of this deficiency in the current management literature, this book is devoted entirely to this timely topic. Not only is the management audit related to the other audits currently employed by business organizations, but more importantly, a complete management audit questionnaire is presented for evaluating the functional areas of a typical organization from a management viewpoint. Specifically, separate sections of the questionnaire are presented for corporate planning, accounting, finance, marketing (including physical distribution), research & development, engineering, manufacturing (including inventory and purchasing), and personnel. Also, sections are set forth for an organization's work environment and its information system. From this perspective, managerial efficiency or lack thereof can be pinpointed. If unfavorable conditions exist, the questionnaire will highlight them and thus provide a starting point for taking remedial action to improve organizational performance.

The principal reason for employing a management audit questionnaire is the need for detecting deficiencies in ongoing operations, a need clearly recognized by business, educational, and government organizations. Although there is an annual review (audit) by outside accountants focusing on "what has happened financially during the past year," the end result is *backward-looking*. What is needed is a *forward-looking* approach that centers on evaluating management's effectiveness in accomplishing organization objectives; performing the management functions of planning, organization, directing, and controlling; and making managerial decisions that

vii

move toward stated plans and objectives. Such an approach is taken in this book by presenting a management audit questionnaire to evaluate managerial performance of its tasks. From this enlightened view, management can more efficiently correct managerial deficiencies *now* instead of waiting for outside auditors to disclose the poor results of past management problems.

The book's structure follows a logical sequence for a *comprehensive* treatment of management audits. Although the questionnaire is developed by functional areas, its structure for the most part consists of (1) long-range plans, (2) short- or medium-range plans, (3) organization structure, (4) leadership, (5) communication, and (6) control, which are the essential functions of management. The specific areas covered are as follows:

Part I: Introduction to Management Auditing. The various types of audits that have been developed over the years, particularly management audits, are reviewed (Chapter 1). Important considerations for undertaking a management audit are then discussed (Chapter 2).

Part II: Management Auditing of Financially Oriented Functional Areas. Those functions that are essential to corporate planning provide a starting basis for the initial sections of the management audit questionnaire (Chapter 3). Next, questions relating to accounting and finance are set forth (Chapter 4). In both chapters, sample case studies of the XYZ Company (to be utilized throughout the text) are presented to illustrate the application of the management audit questionnaire to typical management problems. Also, recommendations are offered on the basis of the evaluation of the facts and the completed section(s) of the questionnaire.

Part III: Management Auditing of Marketing- and Service-Oriented Functional Areas. Sections of the management audit questionnaire are illustrated for the typical areas found in marketing (Chapter 5). In a similar manner, appropriate sections are illustrated for research & development and engineering (Chapter 6). As in Part II, selected case studies of the XYZ Company are presented to illustrate the application of the questionnaire, and recommendations are proposed to solve existing management problems.

Part IV: Management Auditing of Production-Oriented and Personnel Functional Areas. This part follows the same format as the preceding two, that is, sections of a management audit questionnaire are illustrated and applied to a manufacturing environment (Chapter 7). Similarly, detailed questions are set forth for the personnel area, where selected sections are applied to the XYZ Company for resolving managerial deficiencies (Chapter 8).

Part V: Management Auditing of the Work Environment and Information System Areas. Whereas the preceding parts focus on the traditional functional areas of an organization, this final part centers on sections of the questionnaire that relate to the work environment and the human element (Chapter 9) as well as the information system (Chapter 10). These final sections complete a questionnaire as utilized in a comprehensive management audit.

Given its contents, the text should be suitable for a variety of users and purposes. Practitioners, in particular individual managers, will find it helpful for self-evaluation. Consultants and auditors will find practical guidelines for evaluating managerial effectiveness and, on the basis of such an evaluation, making recommendations to overcome managerial (and operational) difficulties. Similarly, the book is suitable as a companion work to accompany a business policy text. In this function, the management audit questionnaire serves as a beginning point for evaluating case studies found in many management or related courses. Additionally, the text is designed for use in management training programs where the major emphasis is to broaden the individual's awareness and understanding of management problems. Thus, the practitioner and the academician will find management auditing through the questionnaire to be of great value in expanding their capabilities to uncover and solve pressing problems facing management.

I wish to thank the following professors at Xavier University who have contributed their many talents to this managerial project: Jerry Anderson, John Camealy, Daniel Geeding, Robert Klekamp, and William Lewis. Also, I want to thank Thomas Gannon of American Management Associations for making this publication possible.

ROBERT J. THIERAUF

Contents

I

INTRODUCTION

to
Management
Auditing

1

Nature and Purpose of a Management Audit

TRADITIONALLY, AUDITING HAS BEEN financially oriented, focusing on the correctness of accounting records and the propriety of activities contained in these records. However, its emphasis has been changing over the years. It is now responding to a demand for more useful information that cannot be found solely in financial statements. In the late 1940s, for example, financial analysts and bankers showed a desire for information suitable for managerial appraisal. Today, stockholders, investors, government bodies, and the general public are seeking information by which the "quality of management" can be judged. As a result of this awakened interest of outsiders in judging the merits of organizations, there has arisen a similar movement from within organizations to judge the results of operations and their managers.

KINDS OF AUDITS

In view of past and emerging directions in auditing, this first chapter will examine its approaches as practiced today. The types of audits to be discussed are:

1. *Financial audit*—performed by internal and external auditors.
2. *Operations audit*—undertaken by internal auditors, operational auditors, external auditors, and management consultants.
3. *Management audit*—performed by internal and external auditors, internal and management consultants, and organization managers.
4. *Performance audit*—undertaken by members of the board of directors.
5. *Social audit*—performed by high-level executives as well as internal and external management consultants.

In succeeding chapters, only the management audit will be discussed in depth. In fact, after setting forth the essentials of management audits and an approach to undertaking a typical management audit in the next chapter, the remainder of the text will be devoted to a comprehensive management audit questionnaire along with typical applications (case studies) for the XYZ Company, a typical manufacturing firm.

Financial Audit

The earliest kind of auditing, and still the most common, was financial. From the viewpoint of the external independent auditors (public accountants and certified public accountants), review and evaluation of a client's accounting and financial reporting system influence the selection and timing of auditing procedures, which ultimately form a basis for the auditor's opinion on the reasonableness of the financial statements. If the review and evaluation by the independent accountants uncover no material discrepancies in the financial statements prepared by the client, the client is given an "unqualified" opinion—that is, the auditors concur that the accounting statements are fair and prepared in conformity with generally accepted accounting principles, consistently applied. However, if there are unresolved important differences, the independent auditors may give a "qualified" opinion or "disclaim" their opinion, depending on the magnitude of the differences.

Internal control, which is of great concern to the independent public accountants, is divided into two categories:

1. *Internal accounting control,* which is designed to bring about the accurate and suitable recording and summarizing of authorized financial transactions.
2. *Internal check,* which is designed to safeguard assets against defalcation or other similar irregularities.

To evaluate internal control, most CPAs use a "Questionnaire for Evaluation of Internal Accounting Control and Internal Check."[1] The questionnaire is designed to pinpoint weak areas of accounting control. All "yes" answers indicate favorable internal control, whereas "no" answers must be explained in writing and indicate a possible weakness in internal control. If the question is not applicable, it is ignored. It should be noted that the letter on internal control is normally issued sometimes after the accountant's opinion has been rendered to the client. This delay is caused by the timing requirements, since the auditor's opinion as to the reasonableness of the financial statements is normally integrated into the client's annual reports to stockholders.

An outgrowth of financial auditing is *internal auditing,* which was originally oriented toward accounting and financial matters. However, in 1957 internal auditing was revised so that its orientation moved toward operations auditing. From this expanded perspective, the overall objectives of internal auditing can be described as an approach to assist financial and operating management and their personnel in accomplishing their tasks. This view is reflected in current thinking and is exemplified in the following statement:

> The concept of internal auditing . . . to an increasing degree . . . is viewed as an arm of management. This development is a product of the modern business environment. The larger and more complex the business organization, the greater is the gap between administrator or executive and the individual operator. Consequently, a sort of liaison is necessary . . . reviews are necessary to keep the business machine functioning smoothly. It is in this area or void that the internal audit is proving to be of value.[2]

From this enlightened view, the internal auditor can fulfill two important functions. He can carry out the traditional role of auditing internal operations that are accounting-oriented. For example, he can audit payroll, receivables, and inventory records that complement and supplement the work of outside auditors. Additionally, he can perform operations audits, the next matter for discussion.

Operations Audit

The operations audit, sometimes referred to as operational audit, has evolved from the financial audit. It goes beyond the accounting functions and treats nonfinancial activities that are ultimately expressed in the organization's accounting records. The purpose of an operations audit is to review and appraise operations and operating procedures. It also involves informing management of operating problems that need to be corrected for greater efficiency and economy of operations. As Corrine Norgaard stated:

> The operational audit examination covers a review of the objectives of the firm, its operating environment, organizational structure, operating plans, and policies, its personnel and physical facilities. These are reviewed in terms of their contribution (or lack of contribution) to operating efficiency or cost savings.[3]

Thus, an operational audit is oriented toward the efficiency of *operational* activities as opposed to strictly *managerial* activities.

In order to ensure that operational areas are studied thoroughly, a questionnaire is used; it acts as a checklist for reviewing and appraising operational methods and procedures. The contrast between the types of questions likely to be used in an operations audit questionnaire and an internal control questionnaire can be seen from the following examples: [4]

OPERATIONS AUDIT QUESTIONNAIRE	INTERNAL CONTROL QUESTIONNAIRE
What are the responsibilities of the head of the purchasing department?	Is the purchasing function completely separated from other functions, particularly accounting and shipping and receiving functions?
What types of reports are prepared in this department?	
How are quantities to be purchased determined?	Are purchase requisitions prepared? Are purchase orders prenumbered?

Not only is an operations audit questionnaire [5] used in this audit approach, but also system flowcharts and process flowcharts are employed to define areas of operations in which management attention can result in the greatest benefit. Time studies are also useful in making systematic observations and increasing the operations auditor's knowledge about the area under study. Tools of the auditor, then, are questionnaires, flowcharts, and time studies, along with the traditional reports, charts, graphs, and manuals.

The end product of every operations audit is a written report to management (like the internal control letter from the outside auditors). This report is advisory and should be interpreted in this light. However, it should emphasize the values that can accrue to the organization from taking appropriate action. The report's focus should be on improving operational practices and procedures, thereby highlighting specific opportunities for cost reduction and improvement of results. Thus, the real purpose of the audit—gauging the effectiveness of operations and discovering opportunities for improving them in the interests of economy or better control—should be an integral part of the final report.

Management Audit

Management audits are concerned with appraising management's accomplishment of organizational objectives; the management functions of planning, organizing, directing, and controlling; and the adequacy of management's decisions and actions in moving toward its stated objectives. Hence, the accent is on evaluating managers' ability to manage.

A management audit should not be confused with "management consulting" or "management advisory services," which deal with all areas of organization performance, including marketing, manufacturing, finance, personnel, and the entire range of organizational functions. The latter are generally directed toward the solution of a specific problem that is known to exist when the management consulting engagement is undertaken. In the solution of a problem, far-reaching organization and/or functional changes are often made and are appropriately considered a part of a management consulting engagement. Differences between management services and management audits can be summarized as follows: [6]

	MANAGEMENT SERVICES	MANAGEMENT AUDITS
Purpose	Assist management.	Appraise management.
Orientation	To the task.	To the individual.
Method	Designed for the specific task.	Designed to permit some standardization, e.g., use of questionnaire and other devices.
Repetition	Seldom—limited to completion of specific task.	Frequent—promote periodic appraisal.
Scope	Toward the specific.	Toward the general as well as the specific.

In addition, a distinction should be made between management audits and operations audits. *Management audits are concerned with the quality of managing,* whereas *operations audits center on the quality of operations.* The basic difference between the two audits, then, is not in method, but in the level of appraisal. As will be noted in the comprehensive management audit questionnaire presented in this text, some of the questions may appear to be of an operational nature. Actually, these questions are appraising the manager's ability to perform his or her assigned tasks. Thus, the two audits are complementary and supplementary to one another.

One of the earliest programs of management auditing was developed by the American Institute of Management, founded and operated by Jackson Martindell. Using an extensive list of 301 questions, Martindell undertook to rate an organization in the areas of economic functions, corporate structure, health of earnings, fairness to stockholders, research & development, directors, fiscal policies, production efficiency, sales vigor, and executive ability.[7] Each of these ten areas was in turn assigned certain point weights. Out of the total of 10,000 possible points, only 3,500 were assigned to managerial elements; the rest were applicable to other areas. Although this early work can be faulted for its high degree of subjectivity and its investor orientation, it did focus on an appraisal of overall management and on results that can be expected from effective management.

Another approach to a management audit was set forth by William

Greenwood, who utilized 203 checkpoints in auditing decisions and 170 in auditing management functions.[8] Even though his 373 questions did not give or imply any standard of what is good or poor, his approach could assist management in getting a comprehensive search analysis of itself and its approach to managing. A comprehensive management audit was also developed by William P. Leonard.[9] Even though this work dealt more with the methods and procedures of an audit, it is valuable in that it indicates what a management audit should cover.

The greatest interest today among those capable of pursuing management audits has been demonstrated by the accounting (audit) firms, in particular the large ones.[10] This interest is only natural since these firms are experienced in financial auditing and management services. The author, who has had considerable experience in various types of audits and general management consulting, finds that the need for appraising management is paramount in all types and sizes of organizations. Because of the importance of this need, this text takes a new and exciting direction in presenting a comprehensive management audit questionnaire.

A summary of the various parts and sections of the management audit questionnaire to be presented in future chapters is found in Figure 1-1. Inspection of the questionnaire's components reveals that the functional areas of a typical manufacturing firm—corporate planning, accounting, finance, marketing, research & development, engineering, manufacturing, and personnel—serve as a basis for evaluating management's capabilities. This comprehensive approach results in a penetrating inquiry into the quality of management. As will be noted in the application of the questionnaire to the XYZ Company's case studies, such an inquiry provides a means for highlighting problems and formulating corrective recommendations to the appropriate management level.

The management audit questionnaire, as illustrated in the text, may be used effectively at all levels in the management hierarchy.[11] A group vice president, for example, may use audits to maintain close contact with various divisions of his group in remote locations. A division manager or a plant manager may also use audits as a control device for his division or plant. No matter what the orientation of the user, the management audit is designed to appraise the effectiveness of management in accomplishing its assigned tasks.

Performance Audit

In many corporations of the past, the board of directors has played a relatively passive role inasmuch as most policy decisions were made by top management.[12] However, because of the rise of consumerism and social re-

Figure 1-1. Summary of the management audit questionnaire.

FINANCIALLY ORIENTED FUNCTIONAL AREAS

Corporate Planning—Chapter 3
    Section I. Overview and Objectives
    Section II. Plans
    Section III. Strategies and Programs
    Section IV. Policies, Procedures, and Standards

Accounting and Finance—Chapter 4
    Section I. Accounting and Finance Overview
    Section II. Accounting
    Section III. Finance

MARKETING- AND SERVICE-ORIENTED FUNCTIONAL AREAS

Marketing—Chapter 5
    Section I. Marketing Overview
    Section II. Sales
    Section III. Market Research
    Section IV. Advertising
    Section V. Physical Distribution

Research & Development and Engineering—Chapter 6
    Section I. Research & Development and
      Engineering Overview
    Section II. Research & Development
    Section III. Engineering

PRODUCTION-ORIENTED AND PERSONNEL FUNCTIONAL AREAS

Manufacturing—Chapter 7
    Section I. Manufacturing Overview
    Section II. Production Planning
    Section III. Production
    Section IV. Inventory
    Section V. Purchasing

Personnel—Chapter 8
    Section I. Personnel Overview
    Section II. Manpower Planning
    Section III. Industrial Relations

WORK ENVIRONMENT AND INFORMATION SYSTEM AREAS

Work Environment and Human Element—Chapter 9
    Section I. Work Structure
    Section II. Informal Structure
    Section III. Control of the Human Element

Information System—Chapter 10
    Section I. Computer Department Controls
    Section II. Input, Programmed, and Output Controls
    Section III. Interactive and Security Controls

sponsibility, there is a new attitude that the board should be more attuned to the dynamic changes taking place. In order to get outside directors more involved in corporate boards on which they serve, there seems to be a trend toward charging outside directors (that is, a subcommittee of non-management directors) with the responsibility of conducting *performance audits*.

The idea that outsiders should play a more active role in reviewing management's performance is not new. Some fifty years ago, Northwestern Mutual Life Insurance Company of Milwaukee adopted bylaws establishing a policyholder examining committee composed of five persons with no relationship to the insurance industry except that they were insured by the company. The committee was empowered to look into any aspect of Northwestern's operations and issue independent reports to the policyholders.[13] Thus, the idea of performance auditing is relatively old, but its implementation on a wide scale is of more recent origin.

Even though the *stated* purpose of a performance audit is to appraise results so that the board can knowledgeably evaluate the strategy and performance objectives which management proposes, its *real* purpose is to create an informed dialog between the president and the directors about the future performance standards for which the president will subsequently be held accountable.[14] Since management and the board can neither predict what will happen in a rapidly changing environment nor control it, standards for future performance are difficult to draw. For this reason, performance standards should be expressed in relative terms. Stating the goal as "increasing our earnings per share by 10 percent per year over the next five years" is not advisable because the result is as much affected by the rate of inflation as by management's performance. A much better statement would be "to increase the earnings rate better than that achieved by 75 percent of the companies in our industry."

The main parts of the audit are concerned with evaluating the quality of management and the quality of corporate citizenship. Because outside directors can never know as much about the business as the company's managers, the focus should be on the quality of the top management team, in particular, the individual and collective quality as well as the quality of managerial processes by which the team works together. The other aspect of the performance audit is the relationship of the organization to its social and political environment. In this capacity, outside directors act as a sort of corporate conscience. Although many corporate board executives are sensitized to current issues of the day, they may not be aware of important issues of the future that could have a far-reaching impact on business. In the final analysis, the performance audit is designed to make more constructive use of outside directors' experience and expertise.

A good example of insufficient involvement of outside directors in corporate matters is the Penn Central debacle.[15] Dozens of lawsuits have been filed by disgruntled shareholders seeking to prove that the duties of prudence and loyalty, if not abdicated, were less than diligently pursued by the Penn Central board prior to the debacle. As one former director admitted, "I don't think anybody was aware that it was that close to collapse."[16] He contends that directors were continually asking for more information from the officers but that "most of our time was spent on approving expenditures for the railroad." There was no audit committee of outside directors to question the accountants about the company's financial status. Such a classic example should be sufficient warning to other corporations.

Social Audit

The social audit, which is an approach for monitoring, appraising, and measuring the social performance of business, dates back as far as 1940. In that year, Theodore J. Kreps, then professor of business economics at Stanford University, wrote a monograph on the measurement of social performance.[17] He presented the findings on 22 industries for a 20-year period from 1919 to 1938 and directed his efforts to the following six measurements:[18]

1. Employment.
2. Production.
3. Consumer effort commanded. (What have consumers been compelled to surrender in exchange for what they get?)
4. Consumer funds absorbed. (What has happened to the stream of dollars which the industry has collected from the public and its customers in exchange for services rendered?)
5. Payrolls.
6. Dividends and interest.

Kreps indicates that his measurements do not constitute an exhaustive audit, for they give no indication of such vitally important facts as percentage of capacity operated, investment outlet provided, opportunity for new entrants, stability of operations, fullness of use of patents, modernization, and the like.

The next important development in the social audit, as conceived by Howard R. Bowen in 1953, was a high-level, independent appraisal conducted about every five years by a group of auditors. The auditors' report would be an evaluation with recommendations intended for internal usage by the directors and the management of the firm audited. Eight areas suggested by Bowen [19] for appraisal were company policies regarding:

1. Prices.
2. Wages.
3. Research & development.
4. Advertising.
5. Public relations.
6. Human relations.
7. Community relations.
8. Employment stabilization.

Many of the advantages that Bowen offered for his form of the social audit are still valid today:

> (1) It would provide a recognized method for bringing the social point of view to the attention of management; (2) the appraisal of individual corporations would be made by persons outside the company who would have a more disinterested and detached view of its activities than company employees; (3) the creation of a specialized group of social auditors would give an impetus to the consideration and development of recognized social standards for corporate practice; (4) the fact that the report on the audit would be made to the company and not to the public would make possible complete frankness and at the same time would make the scheme more acceptable to businessmen. [20]

Though Bowen's version was more related to the modern version of the audit than Kreps's approach, it did not contain any specific applications of the social audit. The pioneering efforts of the social audit came of age in the 1970s. Sethi captures the real essence of such an audit by stating: "At the risk of oversimplification, we might say that the purpose of the social audit is to help break down the broad term 'social responsibility of business' into identifiable components and to develop scales that can measure these components." [21]

Bauer and Fenn, pioneers in the development of modern forms of social auditing, take it to mean "a commitment to systematic assessment of and reporting on some meaningful, definable domain of a company's activities that have social impact." [22] There are other definitions representing differing points of view. Similarly, considerable differences of opinion exist over what topics should be covered by such an audit, what criteria should be employed for measurement, whether the audit should be done by internal or external auditors, and whether the results of the audit should be for internal management use only or for general publication. Numerous individuals and consultants are experimenting with forms of the social audit and are assisting business firms in the implementation of these preliminary approaches. Their methodologies and experiences are currently being cited in the literature. George Steiner presents an overview of current business practices concerning the social audit through a survey of 750 corporations.[23]

According to the differing views about social audits, they have multiple motives, which include satisfying the corporate conscience, increasing the wisdom of social programs, improving public relations, and enhancing the credibility of the business firm. From this perspective, a number of social issues are examined:[24]

Minority employment.
Pollution/environment.
Working conditions.
Community relations.
Philanthropic contributions.
Consumerism issues.

Since there is little precedent for conducting a social audit, four general approaches have been suggested[25] for reporting their results:

1. *The inventory approach*—a list of all of the company's social activities is prepared.
2. *The cost or outlay approach*—in addition to the list of social activities, the amount spent on each activity is disclosed.
3. *The program management approach*—in addition to the information disclosed by the cost or outlay approach, a statement is made as to whether or not the company met its objectives for each activity.
4. *The benefit–cost approach*—in addition to the information disclosed by the cost or outlay approach, the real worth, that is, the benefit of each expenditure, is indicated.

The least informative of these approaches is the inventory approach, but the current state of the art results in its being used by most firms that have chosen to report on their social activities. The most informative approach is the benefit–cost approach, but the benefits are extremely difficult to measure given the current state of the art. The program management approach is a reasonable substitute for the benefit–cost approach and is used by the General Accounting Office in its audit of government agencies. However, probably few companies have formulated objectives regarding their social activities. Thus, a good approach for an initial attempt at a social audit report would be the cost or outlay approach.[26]

To summarize the foregoing discussion, the various types of audits and their essential characteristics are:

Financial audit—designed to check on the fairness of the accounting statements as prepared in conformity with generally accepted accounting principles, consistently applied.

Operations audit—utilized to review and appraise the efficiency and economy of operating methods and procedures of the organization.

Management audit—concerned with the evaluation of how well management is accomplishing its objectives; performing the managerial functions of planning, organizing, directing, and controlling; and reaching effective decisions in accomplishing stated organization objectives.

Performance audit—employed to determine the quality of the top management team that makes the key decisions in the organization as well as the quality of its cooperation in accomplishing organization objectives.

Social audit—concerned not only with reporting the organization's involvement in socially oriented activities, but also with determining whether or not it has met its objectives for each activity.

As indicated earlier, the financial audit is supplemented by newer forms of audits, in particular management audits—the subject matter of this text.

THE MANAGEMENT AUDIT QUESTIONNAIRE

By way of review, a management audit questionnaire aims at a comprehensive and constructive examination of an organization's management and its assigned tasks. Overall, the questionnaire is concerned with the appraisal of management actions in accomplishing organization objectives. Its primary objective is to highlight weaknesses and deficiencies of the organization for possible improvements. More specifically, it includes a review of how well or badly the managerial functions of planning, organizing, directing, and controlling are being performed. In addition, it evaluates how effective the decision-making process is in accomplishing stated organization objectives. Within this framework, the questionnaire provides a means for evaluating an organization's ongoing operations by examining its major functional areas.

Before discussing the benefits and problems of undertaking a management audit, it is important to understand what the questionnaire is designed to accomplish. It does not provide answers; it simply asks questions. The questions are asked to help bridge the gap between management *theory* and *practice*. To better understand this distinction, consider the origins of management theory. In general, theory originated from two sources. The early theory tended to be "normative." In effect, practitioners and observers of management discipline reflected upon the managerial practices that they had used and observed in various organizations and synthesized this experience into management principles, that is, management theory. Because these observations were personal, the principles tended to be subjective. More recent theory has grown out of controlled experimentation. Using the methodology of the behavioral scientists, researchers carefully studied, and continue to study, the world of the manager. The results, within the boundaries of the experimentation, tend to be more objective. However, we are still dealing with management theory.

In either case, whether personal observation or controlled experimentation is the source, any principle tends to focus on the managerial process and to ignore the environmental considerations involved. Thus, a principle, being a fundamental truth, transcends the specific and moves to the universal. Herein lies the problem. Every manager must deal with a specific situation when involved in managerial problem solving. Hence, the questions that are asked within the various sections of the management audit questionnaire are designed to aid the manager to sort out those factors, forces, and effects that are relevant to the situation being studied. From this viewpoint, the questionnaire is designed to evaluate management practices.

As will be seen throughout this text, there are three possible answers to the management audit questions: "yes," "no," and "N.A." (not applicable). A "yes" answer indicates that the specific area, function, or aspect under study is functioning in an acceptable manner; no written explanation is needed in that case. On the other hand, a "no" answer indicates unacceptable performance and should be explained in writing. Questionnaire comments on negative answers not only provide documentation for future reference, but, more important, provide background information for undertaking remedial action. Those questions that are not applicable and should be ignored in the audit are checked in the "N.A." column.

In any case, these questions are designed to help an individual evaluate real-world situations. As such, the questions should be approached from a research-oriented frame of reference. As stated earlier, use of the questionnaire may not give the answers to problems confronting the organization; its purpose is to help define problems in terms of the specific situations in which they exist. This should be apparent in the case studies of the XYZ Company presented in the text.

BENEFITS OF A MANAGEMENT AUDIT

The principal reason for undertaking a management audit is the need for detecting and overcoming current managerial deficiencies (and resulting operational problems) in ongoing operations. Unlike the annual review by outside accountants, which focuses on the financial results of the past year and thus is *backward-looking,* a management audit represents a more positive, *forward-looking* approach that evaluates how well management accomplishes its stated organization objectives; how effective management is in planning, organizing, directing, and controlling the organization's activities; and how appropriate management's decisions are for reaching stated organization objectives. This evaluation of managerial performance is achieved with the aid of a management audit questionnaire. Whether management evaluation through use of the questionnaire is performed by an outside auditing or consulting firm, the consulting staff within the organization, or selected members of the organization is immaterial. The important point is that some group is charged with the responsibility to undertake this evaluation process periodically.

One benefit of the management audit, then, is that managerial problems and related operational difficulties can be spotted before the fact rather than after the fact as with a financial audit. This forward-looking approach is analogous to the preventive maintenance concept found in production; that is, periodic management audits can pinpoint problems as they are developing from a small scale. In comparison, detecting the same problems at a later time, when they have generally increased in scope, results in higher costs to the organization.

A second important benefit of management auditing is that it represents another management tool to assist the organization in accomplishing desired objectives. The capability of the management audit questionnaire to pinpoint important problem areas that are related to managing an organization is a real plus factor for its use. Business failures are caused largely by poor management. What better way can this important problem be overcome than by employing management audits in an objective manner? If certain managers are ineffective in their present positions, appropriate corrective action should be taken.

Another benefit of management auditing by audit questionnaire is that this approach results in an objective appraisal rather than a subjective one that is based on personal opinion and unsupported by factual evidence. As in most appraisal work, the best results are obtained by using an objective frame of reference. Although judgment in management auditing is an important part in recommending certain courses to improve the present situation, judgment becomes valuable only after the important facts have been compared to some relevant standard, the management audit questionnaire.

SOME PROBLEMS OF MANAGEMENT AUDITS

Like any management tool, management audits must be understood and used properly for satisfactory results. Furthermore, they need the full backing of top management. Two of their principal constraints are the time needed to undertake them and their costs. Because a manager must be advised about pertinent deficiencies, management audits should be performed regularly so that managerial (and operational) problems can be caught before they become overwhelming. Likewise, the costs of undertaking such audits should be budgeted like other organizational expenses so that they are always under control.

Going beyond the time and cost factors, the most important problem of management auditing is that it might negatively affect a manager's morale, which could adversely affect the productivity of his or her area of responsibility and accountability. Utmost tact and diplomacy are required on the part of the evaluator—that is, the consultant, auditor, or reviewing manager—or the management audit will cause dysfunctional effects on those reviewed. Thus, "the people problem" emerges as the most critical factor in undertaking a management audit.

SUMMARY

In this chapter, the various types of audits, namely, financial, operations, management, performance, and social, were discussed. Although there are several kinds of audits to evaluate the practices of management, the focus in this text is on the "management audit" through use of the *management audit questionnaire*. The management audit can serve a vital purpose by providing an objective, impartial, and competent appraisal of managerial activities as well as a means for continuously redirecting the firm's efforts toward constantly changing plans and objectives. In addition, management audits evaluate the plans, the organization structure, and the directions that management gives in the form of strategies, programs, policies, procedures, and standards. Fundamentally, a management audit through use of the management audit questionnaire provides a means for evaluating the *quality* of management in terms of its ability to manage and accomplish desired organization objectives; to perform the planning, organizing, directing, and controlling functions; and to reach effective decisions in accomplishing stated organization objectives.

REFERENCES

1. See Philip L. Defliese, Kenneth P. Johnson, and Roderick K. Macleod, *Montgomery's Auditing,* 9th ed. (New York: The Ronald Press Company, 1975), Chapter 3, for more information on the questionnaire. For a typical internal control questionnaire, see ibid., 8th ed., Appendix, pp. 643–704.
2. J. Brooks Heckert and James D. Wilson, *Controllership,* New York: The Ronald Press, 1967, p. 671.
3. Corrine Norgaard, "The Professional Accountant's View of Operational Auditing," *Journal of Accountancy,* December 1969, p. 46.

4. Ibid., p. 47.
5. For a typical operations audit questionnaire, see Roy A. Lindberg and Theodore Cohn, *Operations Auditing*, New York: AMACOM, 1972, pp. 213–294.
6. John W. Buckley, "Management Services and Management Audits by Professional Accountants," *California Management Review*, Fall 1966, p. 44.
7. Jackson Martindell, *The Scientific Appraisal of Management*, New York: Harper & Row, 1962; and *Manual of Excellent Managements*, New York: American Institute of Management, 1957.
8. William T. Greenwood, *A Management Audit System*, rev. ed., Carbondale, Ill.: School of Business, Southern Illinois University, 1967; and *Business Policy: A Management Audit Approach*, New York: Macmillan, 1967.
9. William P. Leonard, *The Management Audit*, Englewood Cliffs, N.J.: Prentice-Hall, 1962.
10. John C. Burton, "Management Auditing," *The Journal of Accountancy*, May 1968, pp. 41–46; and A. E. White, "Management Auditing: The Present State of the Art," *The Journal of Accountancy*, August 1967, pp. 54–58.
11. Olin C. Snellgrave, "The Management Audit: Organizational Guidance System," *Management Review*, March 1972, p. 42.
12. "The Board: It's Obsolete Unless Overhauled," *Business Week*, May 22, 1971, pp. 50–58.
13. Frazar B. Wilde and Richard F. Vancil, "Performance Audits by Outside Directors," *Harvard Business Review*, July–August 1972, pp. 112–113.
14. Ibid., p. 114.
15. Kenneth R. Andrews, "Can the Best Corporations Be Made Moral?" *Harvard Business Review*, May–June, 1973, p. 63.
16. "The Board: It's Obsolete Unless Overhauled," loc. cit., pp. 50–51.
17. Theodore J. Kreps, *Measurement of the Social Performance of Business: An Investigation of Concentration of Economic Power*, Monograph No. 7, Temporary National Economic Committee, Washington, D.C.: U.S. Government Printing Office, 1940.
18. Ibid., pp. 3–5.
19. Howard R. Bowen, *Social Responsibility of the Businessman*, New York: Harper & Row, 1953, p. 155.
20. Ibid., p. 156.
21. Prakash S. Sethi, "Getting a Handle on the Social Audit," *Business and Society Review/Innovation*, Winter 1972–1973, p. 33.
22. Raymond A. Bauer and Don H. Fenn, "What Is a Corporate Social Audit?" *Harvard Business Review*, January–February 1973, p. 38.
23. George A. Steiner, *Summary Results of Survey of Developing Efforts to Measure the Social Performance of Business*, New York: Committee for Economic Development, 1974; and John J. Carson and George A. Steiner, *Measuring Business's Social Performance: The Corporate Social Audit*, New York: Committee for Economic Development, 1975.
24. Archie B. Carroll and George W. Beiler, "Landmarks in the Evolution of the Social Audit," *Academy of Management Journal*, September 1975, pp. 596–598.
25. Steven C. Dilley and Jerry J. Weygandt, "Measuring Social Responsibility: An Empirical Test," *Journal of Accountancy*, September 1973, p. 63.
26. David F. Fetyko, "The Company Social Audit," *Management Accounting*, April 1975.

2

Undertaking
a
Management Audit

IN THE COMING DECADE, there will be an increasing demand for information about managerial performance. This may well manifest itself in additional formal requirements, such as a demand for some impartial evaluation of management performance beyond that implicitly provided by historical results reported in conformity with generally accepted accounting principles.

This demand for evaluating management will probably come from several sources. Investment analysts today recognize that the evaluation of management performance is of crucial importance and, at the same time, extremely difficult for an outsider to undertake; thus they may require management to submit more data on this subject. Similarly, stockholders who control small to large holdings want assurance that their capital is being used effectively. Finally, there is an increasing tendency for the public to feel that corporate management has not only an economic but a social responsibility to use assets under its control effectively.

If outside consultants and auditors are asked to attest not only to financial results but also to the quality and effectiveness of management, it is important to examine the nature of the *management audit* and how it should be undertaken. In this chapter, the considerations prior to conducting a management audit, specifically, its scope, staffing, and frequency, are discussed. The essential aspects of conducting an audit—gathering the facts through interviews and measuring performance through a management audit questionnaire—are set forth, followed by its concluding parts. These entail an oral presentation of recommendations, which is followed by a written report. Lastly, alternative approaches to management auditing and common difficulties experienced in undertaking this type of auditing are enumerated.

As noted previously, there is need for evaluating management's ability to accomplish organization objectives; to perform the planning, organizing, directing, and controlling functions; and to reach effective decisions in accomplishing stated organization objectives. Hence, a truly effective management audit must be a comprehensive and constructive examination of an organization or some part of it to determine managerial (and operational) problems, defects, and irregularities and to indicate recommendations for improvement.

Inasmuch as today's managers are a good deal more than passive custodians of the past, they can and should modify the decisions they inherit. Indeed, to change these decisions when they go wrong, as many decisions are likely to do, is one of their most important and difficult assignments. But today's executives are also charged with the responsibility for shaping the future of the business—with lead times that are becoming increasingly longer and in some areas range up to ten years or more. Performance of management, then, means doing a good job in preparing today's business for the future. This is now referred to as "management by perception." And this is an area in which measurement of managerial performance—or at least an appraisal of it—is needed the most.

The utilization of a management audit questionnaire to evaluate managerial (and operational) performance currently and in the future has several important benefits outside of the actual performance of the audit itself. First, it helps depersonalize the audit by visually signaling the fact that there is form to the audit—and where there is form, there is generally equal treatment. From this view, organization personnel who are interviewed will not be tempted to feel that they have been singled out for investigation. Second, the questionnaire offers a basis for developing audit time standards. The questionnaire involves a specific amount of work, and the time involved in completing it can be used as a measure of the amount of time needed to do the audit next time. Third and last, the questionnaire forces management to deal with its audit in a practical way.

To assist in evaluating management capabilities, many probing questions, as part of a management audit questionnaire, are set forth in future chapters for each functional area of an organization. From an overview standpoint, they focus on important items that determine an individual's managerial success. Fundamentally, they can be summarized in the form of the following questions:

- Do you have the ability to see things clearly from the organization's viewpoint, divorced from personal prejudices and needs?
- Can you pinpoint a problem in your field of responsibility before serious trouble occurs?

- Do you encourage others to air their opinions, and are you responsive to their viewpoints?
- Are you willing to take a chance now and then to further organization objectives?
- Can you simplify questions and cut problems down to size?
- Can you present yourself and your beliefs so as to influence people and move them toward a desired goal or objective?
- Is your discipline fair so that subordinates know what to expect of you?

A positive answer to these questions indicates that the manager is capable of managing his or her respective area—or, to state it another way, that he or she is a successful executive and leader of organization personnel.

PRELIMINARY CONSIDERATIONS

Like any other audit, a management audit must be carefully *planned*. Questions such as what specific approach should be used and who will be responsible for performing it must be resolved. Should the management audit be comprehensive or cover only part of an organization? Should it be undertaken by the internal consulting group or auditors, or should outside consultants or auditors be engaged on a periodic basis? Additionally, what are the controlling and limiting factors of the management audit? And what means will be established to appraise performance? The answers to these questions will provide a starting point to selecting the best approach for the organization or area to be studied.

Scope

As indicated previously, a management audit can be comprehensive or it can encompass part of an organization. Most management audit groups from within or outside an organization can handle engagements of any size provided they have enough qualified personnel. Likewise, they can perform management (and operational) evaluations in almost any functional area of the organization if allowed to do so.

When focusing on one functional area, the management audit can center specifically on corporate planning, accounting, finance, marketing, research & development, engineering, manufacturing, or personnel. Similarly, it can focus on the work environment and the human element plus a complete evaluation of the information system. Within the foregoing classification (which, it should be noted, provides the basis for the management audit questionnaire presented in this book), specialized areas may be explored, including sales, market research, advertising, physical distribution, production planning, production, inventory, purchasing, manpower planning, industrial relations, the work environment, or the informal environment structure. Controls relating to computer center operations, input, programs, output, interaction, or security can also be evaluated.

Another way of determining the scope of a management audit is to concentrate on one or more of management's basic functions, namely, planning, organizing, directing, and controlling. In fact, the book is structured so as to allow such selective audits by function. In Chapter 3, the planning function is addressed; in particular, the questions on objectives, plans, strategies, programs, policies, procedures, and standards are set forth from an overview standpoint. In Chapters 4 through 8 on the functional areas, the major questionnaire subsections can be used to evaluate managerial capabilities from this view. Specifically, sections A (long-range plans) and B (short- or medium-range plans) refer to the planning function; section C (organization structure) is concerned with the organizing function; sections D (leadership) and E (communication) involve directing; and, finally, section F (control) applies to management's control function.

Still another approach to management auditing is to limit the evaluation to a certain level of management—lower, middle, or top management. This may be appropriate when problems are being experienced at these levels. For example, if the company is losing its market share to more progressive firms, this may indicate that top management is not taking the initiative to stay with the times. On the other hand, day-to-day operational problems may be indicative of inefficient managers at the lower levels of an organization.

Overall, the question of the scope of a management audit should be viewed from the standpoint of a cost/benefit analysis. If the benefits far outweigh their costs, there is no question that the management audit should be undertaken. If the reverse is true, there is no need for such an audit. To increase the potential benefits from management auditing, it is suggested that the scope of the investigation be broadened. The rationale is that solutions as well as their resulting benefits tend to be larger in scope when the scope of the audit is enlarged.

Staffing

One important source for staffing is internal consultants and auditors. Since most medium- and large-size organizations have their own consulting staffs, a logical starting point would be to engage this group. Comprehensive management audits call for senior internal consultants of broad experience who have a working knowledge of the functional areas to be audited. Also, it is advisable to employ the services of junior internal consultants who will work under the direction of their seniors. In this manner, the expertise and capabilities of both junior and senior internal consultants can be utilized to their fullest. Additionally, it is recommended that the talents of senior internal auditors be used to supplement the internal consultants. The inclusion of internal auditors allows specific operational problems to be reviewed along with managerial problems so that more comprehensive recommendations can be made by the internal consultants and auditors.

If the organization lacks competent consultants and auditors or the staff is too busy on other engagements, it is advisable to engage the services of outside consultants and auditors. The international and national consulting as well as CPA firms are prime sources for undertaking such an audit. Inasmuch as companies are audited by CPA firms, the latter's management consulting service staffs are a natural for undertaking management audits since they can be assisted by the CPAs who have conducted the annual financial audit. In this manner, their combined expertise can be employed to evaluate managerial (and operational) efficiency or lack thereof. In a somewhat similar manner, management consulting firms are prime candidates for conducting management audits. Overall, the determination of who will conduct the audit may be dependent upon the availability of consultants and auditors within as well as outside the organization.

Frequency

Having specified various approaches to a management audit, including its scope and its staffing requirements, the last item that should be considered before undertaking such an audit is its frequency. Prime consideration should be given to the nature of the organization. Is the company in a fast-changing industry where there is great accent on the latest technology in the company's products and/or services? When the organization is subject to rapid change or the total resources utilized are expensive, the frequency of management auditing should be greater than when it does not undergo rapid changes or the resources employed are not high in value. In essence, management audits should be made often enough to provide protection against growing problems. On the other hand, they should not be so frequent as to lead to repetitious results of questionable value.

To get an idea of the optimum frequency of such an audit, it might be worthwhile to look at financial audits. Customarily, financial audits are conducted annually. They are highly programmed, since an internal control questionnaire is utilized to attest to accounting methods and procedures. By contrast, a management audit should be considered from a longer time frame. For an organization that is subject to rapid changes or consumes a great amount of high-cost resources, a two-year basis might be adequate to protect it from managerial and operational problems becoming entrenched or too large. For those organizations in a relatively stable industry, the frequency of the audit can be every three years. In no case should the interval be allowed to exceed three years.

CONDUCTING A MANAGEMENT AUDIT

Once top management has decided on the scope, the staffing, and the frequency of the management audit, the next phase is the undertaking of the actual audit. This involves investigating and analyzing the present facts through interviews as well as completing a management audit questionnaire so as to determine the problems confronting the organization.

Getting the Facts through Interviews

To avoid wasted time and effort, adequate preparation is necessary in management auditing, just as in financial auditing. The management auditors should know what information is desired, and they should be prepared to ask a number of direct questions to get the desired information. Reference can be made to the management audit questionnaire for specific questions.

Care must be taken in selecting the proper managers to interview so as to obtain pertinent information. Needless to say, the persons to be interviewed must be notified beforehand, and they should be informed what reports, records, or other documentation should be available at the time of the interview. Following the foregoing interview procedures will provide the management auditors with the pertinent information that is necessary for a successful management audit.

In the interview itself, the auditors should begin by stating the purpose of the audit. Emphasis should be placed on getting the facts that are essential to review and appraise the functional area(s) under study. The exchange between auditor and manager should be friendly and conducted in an open atmosphere so as to encourage a free exchange of ideas. The manager's opinions on different items should be allowed to be expressed. Of course, they will be disregarded in the report and in subsequent discussions with other company managers if so desired by the manager. It is important that the auditors be tactful and diplomatic at all times. Failure on this one point may result in the management auditors getting only part of the desired information.

In my consulting experience, I found it wise to listen to tentative solutions set forth by the manager for problems that confront him or her. Many times these solutions can be made an integral part of final recommendations, and when the manager sees that his or her solutions are included in the final report, the individual is more apt to support the recommendations. Thus, the management auditors will experience less opposition at the end of the engagement by utilizing this approach.

Also, during the interview, the management auditors should not commit themselves, nor should any recommendations be set forth at this time. Once all pertinent information has been extracted from the interview, it is advisable to verify the accuracy of the information by requesting the person interviewed to read the notes taken and place his or her initials thereon. This extra step makes the individual feel an important part of the management audit.

Measuring Performance through the Management Audit Questionnaire

During the interview, the management auditors make a careful inquiry into the important facts. The next step is to analyze this information, with the aim of measuring current performance. The best way to perform such an analysis is to utilize the sections of the management audit questionnaire that apply to the areas under study.

As noted in the previous chapter, the management audit questionnaire does not give answers, but simply asks questions. If all questions are answered with a yes, operations are proceeding as desired. On the other hand, if there are one or more no answers, difficulties are being experienced and must be explained in writing. If the question does not apply, the N.A. (not applicable) column is checked. Thus, the management audit questionnaire for this part of the audit not only serves as a management tool to analyze the current situation; more importantly, it enables the management auditors to *synthesize* those elements that are causing organizational difficulties and deficiencies. To state it another way, a synthesis (a process of combining separate elements) can be used for determining the problem. The capability to assess all negative answers goes a long way toward defining the real problem—not just stating its symptoms. This should be apparent in the case studies of the XYZ Company presented in the remaining chapters.

Fundamentally, the management audit questionnaire presented in this book includes the following types of questions:

- Are organization *objectives* and derivative *plans* feasible and realistic?
- Are organization *strategies, programs, policies,* and the like, as set forth by management, in conformity with organization objectives and plans?

- Is the *organization structure* capable of carrying out organization objectives?
- Is there adequate managerial *leadership* to accomplish organization objectives?
- Is there adequate *communication* (upward and downward) for management to accomplish organization objectives?
- Are managerial *controls* adequate for accomplishing organization objectives?
- Are there managerial and operational problems relating to the *work environment?*
- Are there managerial problems associated with the *human element?*
- Is the *information system* adequate and working effectively to meet organization objectives?

These overview questions relate to the managerial functions of planning, organizing, directing, and controlling. In turn, they provide an underlying structure for more specific questions that assist in determining the real problems.

Once the real problems, difficulties, and deficiencies have been diagnosed, the management auditors are ready to assess the level of performance for the function or area being investigated—that is, is it excellent, good, fair, poor, bad, or indifferent? Many times, the performance is far below expectations. This means that many recommendations will be in order to overcome below-average performance. This is an important part of concluding a management audit—the subject matter of the next section.

CONCLUDING A MANAGEMENT AUDIT

The preparation of the management audit report that covers the details of the management auditors' findings and recommendations represents an important part of concluding an audit assignment. To assist in the preparation of the final report, the management auditors normally meet with management and other concerned personnel for the purpose of discussing freely any aspect or finding of the audit. This approach assists the independent third party in bringing together the important elements of the audit as well as determining appropriate recommendations. Also, it will disclose any ''hang-ups'' that organization personnel may have toward a particular solution. It is far better to discuss alternative recommendations and feel out the possible consequences of recommended action. In this way, when corrective actions are undertaken, the resulting consequences can be predicted, thereby avoiding unworkable solutions.

Because of the importance of the oral presentation of recommendations and the final report to management, these areas are covered in some depth below. However, it should be noted that the type of report required varies with the level of investigation. Thus, a comprehensive investigation involves a report that is very broad in scope, while a smaller-scale investigation of one or two functional areas will result in a less comprehensive report.

Oral Recommendations for Improvement

From a management viewpoint, the main focus of the audit is recommendations. Generally, there is an oral presentation of specific recommendations to the members of the top management team who approved the audit. In some cases, the approval may have come from the board of directors, which then becomes the recipient of the auditors' oral recommendations. Upon completion of the presentation, oral recommendations become an integral part of the final report—the subject matter for the next section.

In the oral presentation, recommendations representing feasible solutions that will be accepted without too much difficulty are discussed initially. This gives the management auditors an opportunity to establish their credibility. The auditors should back these recommendations with a cost/benefit analysis that indicates the expected return to the organization from implementing them. Where implementation may be difficult because of personality problems, organizational changes, and the like, the auditors should still push their proposals if their benefits exceed their costs. In essence, those recommendations that are necessary to assist in fulfilling organization objectives in a more efficient and economical manner should be presented for implementation. However, it should be noted that if certain recommendations are not accepted during the oral presentation, it is wise to offer alternatives. In the consulting profession, this is known as the "escape route." In other words, "cover your tracks" and "be prepared at all times."

An integral part of the oral presentation is determining when and where the recommendations can be put into operation. The interchange of ideas among management and the auditors allows for a logical development of appropriate dates for implementation. Additionally, it assists the management auditors in drawing up an implementation timetable for inclusion in their final report.

Preparation of a Management Audit Report

As indicated previously, the content and length of the management audit report will vary from audit to audit. The important factors are the scope of the audit, the competence of management, the explicit terms of the engagement, and the recommendations of the audit. In any case, the report should contain certain essential elements, detailed below and in Figure 2-1.

First, there should be a section stating the purpose and scope of the engagement. This must include a description of the functional areas or managerial functions and activities covered in the audit. Areas of management activities that are not covered and for which the management auditors assume no responsibility, expressed or implied, should also be described. These could include such items as managerial forecasts of earnings and projections of the results of plans and strategies in future years.

The second part contains a statement describing the management auditing procedures the auditors found appropriate and used in the engagement. In particular, this part may describe appropriate sections of the management audit questionnaire set forth in the remaining chapters. Also included in this part are any limitations made or encountered during the course of the audit engagement.

The third part of the report centers on a discussion of the important facts surrounding managerial and operational problems. This discussion should be as factual and objective as possible so that there is no misunderstanding of what the management auditors intended. Also, attendant circumstances—that is, detrimental conditions, deficiencies of operation, and irregularities—should be an integral part of the discussion. Overall, the discussion in this third part should be arranged in a manner that provides a proper balance between clarity and brevity; also, the various facts and problems should be presented in order of their importance.

Moving on to the fourth part of the report, appropriate recommendations are detailed. In general, recommendations should be presented in the order of their acceptability. To state it another way, recommendations that have greater chances of acceptance should be set forth first, followed by ones that may be of lesser interest to management. If at all possible, recommendations should be accompanied by cost/benefit analyses indicating to what extent the organization would benefit from their implementation. In addition, recommendations should be offered with the appropriate caveats and, where necessary, with alternative recommendations. Finally, there should be a timetable contained in the report for implementing the recommendations.

The last part contains the *attestation,* that is, a brief statement setting forth the auditor's evaluation of management performance during the period under audit. It should be worded so that it is quite clear that the auditor's evaluation is a matter of judgment, based primarily on the evidence obtained in the investigation. Also, this final part should include a denial of any responsibility for the activities of the company's management or the results—past, present, or future—of operations. An example of the attestation is shown in Figure 2-2.

Figure 2-1. The major parts of a typical management audit report.

OUTLINE—CONTENTS OF MANAGEMENT AUDIT REPORT

Part I.   Purpose and Scope of the Management Audit—centers on the reason for undertaking the audit and the functional areas or managerial functions evaluated.

Part II.   Management Auditing Procedures Utilized—focuses on the utilization of the appropriate sections of the management audit questionnaire (as set forth in Chapters 3 through 10) as well as limitations made or encountered in the audit.

Part III. Discussion of Important Facts and Problems—a thorough discussion of the facts related to the real problem. There should be a proper balance between clarity and brevity in the report.

Part IV.   Appropriate Recommendations to Overcome Problems—centers on making recommendations that are backed by favorable cost/benefit analyses. Also, alternative recommendations are offered if certain recommendations may be somewhat controversial. A timetable for implementing the recommendations is incorporated in the report.

Part V.   Management Auditors' Evaluation of Managerial Performance—sets forth the opinion of the management auditors on the capabilities of management in the areas investigated.

Regarding this last part, the management auditors are not expressly professing or implying infallibility, but simply expressing an opinion. Another group of auditors might reach a different conclusion from the same evidence and, consequently, express a different opinion. It also should be evident that one may find fault later with the auditor's judgment in light of information that was not available at the time of the audit. However, if due professional care is used, the variations should not exceed those attributed to normal sampling errors.

ALTERNATIVE APPROACHES TO A MANAGEMENT AUDIT

The foregoing represents a *comprehensive* approach to management auditing that is employed by external or internal consultants and auditors. Usually, a management audit is undertaken on a periodic basis, say every two or three

Figure 2-2. A typical management auditor's opinion
to be included in the final part of the management audit report.

MANAGEMENT AUDITOR'S OPINION
To the Board of Directors and Top Management
of the XYZ Company

We have investigated the management of the XYZ Company for the period ended December 31, (Year). In carrying out our investigation, we focused on the following areas:

(to be filled in on the basis of the audit's scope)

In conducting our investigation and evaluating managerial performance, we used management auditing procedures and available standards which we considered necessary and appropriate in the circumstances. More specifically, a management audit questionnaire was employed for evaluating managerial performance.

Based upon the major findings and recommendations found in the prior part of this report, in our judgment, the XYZ Company was managed with reasonable efficiency as of December 31, (Year), judged in the light of our findings and the circumstances in which the company operated. Additionally, it should be understood that our firm assumes no responsibility for the activities of the company's management or the results of operations.

February 10, (Year)   Progressive Consulting Company
                                       Management Consultants and Auditors

---

years. The nature of the company and its products and services, as indicated previously, determines the frequency of the audit. Overall, this chapter has stressed a periodic approach to management auditing.

As will be noted in the two sample applications of the XYZ Company in the chapters to follow, this approach is not used there. The intent of these case studies is to demonstrate how the various sections of the management audit questionnaire can be applied to organization problems. As any manager knows, in the real business world specific problems arise unexpectedly. Hence, there is a need to investigate them immediately rather than according to some predetermined schedule, and this is the approach taken for the various case studies of the XYZ Company.

Inasmuch as selected sections of the management audit questionnaire are applied to the XYZ Company, generally consultants and auditors from within and outside the XYZ Company are employed to solve the problems through specific recommendations. This approach results in a third-party view, which makes for an objective evaluation of the area being investigated.

In addition to the *comprehensive* approach to management auditing set forth in the chapter and the *selective* approach illustrated in the XYZ Company case studies, there is another approach to management auditing. This is the application of one or more sections (or parts) of the questionnaire by the manager to the area under his or her jurisdiction. Although this approach results in a *subjective* rather than objective evaluation, it nevertheless is a valid one. It indicates that a particular manager wants to know where specific problem areas are and what can be done to overcome them. In a few words, the manager is aggressive and wants to be on top of the situation rather than spend a lot of his or her time ''putting out fires.'' Perhaps the greatest utilization of the management audit questionnaire will come from managers who desire a comprehensive evaluation tool for areas under their command and control.

Overall, the three approaches—comprehensive/objective, selective/objective, and selective/subjective—to management auditing may prove to start a new revolution in managerial performance. Management auditing is capable of raising the level of efficiency and economy of organizational operations, with the end result that organization objectives will be more fully realized.

COMMON DIFFICULTIES ENCOUNTERED IN A MANAGEMENT AUDIT

During the course of a management audit, various difficulties will commonly arise. One big difficulty is the reluctance of managers to make the changes that were accepted during the oral presentation. Usually, the main reason is that organization personnel under them like the status quo and thus resist change. What may have been quite logical to management at the time of the oral presentation may still be, except that management is having second thoughts about implementing the recommendations because of the people problem.

To overcome resistance at the implementation stage may prove to be a trying experience for any executive. This unfortunate situation can be avoided by taking a positive approach to management auditing, as set forth earlier in the chapter. This means getting the various people involved in the management audit who will be implementing the final recommendations. By making their ideas an integral part of the auditor's recommendations, the resistance to change is substantially reduced. Thus, it behooves management to get certain organization personnel involved from the start in the management audit.

Perhaps the most traumatic experience for organization executives is the removal of incompetent managers on the basis of the auditors' final recommendations. The recommendation may be that one or more individuals be asked to resign, or that certain individuals be removed from their positions and transferred to jobs of lesser importance. Clearly, a reshuffling of management can have a decidedly negative impact on any organization. It is far better to make the changes now rather than later when the firm may be fighting for its life because of the incompetence of its managers. An organization is better able to absorb the shock of a management change when it is operating profitably than when it is losing money. Needless to say, it is difficult to attract good managers when the organization is operating in troubled waters.

Another common difficulty encountered in a management audit, from its inception to its implementation, is getting sufficient time from the organization's managers. Too often, these executives are out of the office for one reason or another, resulting in unforeseen delays of the audit. If all managers know that the engagement has the backing of the board of directors and top management, there is less likely to be a problem in this area. In general, the management auditors should allow for this problem to a reasonable degree, since this is how the real world operates. However, unreasonable delays that are caused by managers "dragging their feet" should be reported promptly to the executive who can rectify the situation.

Summary

The "manager for all seasons" of today recognizes that *management auditing* is a managerial tool, instrumental in evaluating and determining his or her quality of performance. It is also an instrument for measuring the effectiveness of an organization's functional areas—in particular, how effective management is in accomplishing desired objectives; how well the managerial functions of planning, organizing, directing, and controlling are being performed; and how effective management is in reaching appropriate decisions to accomplish stated organization objectives in the functional areas. A properly executed management audit, then, is an excellent means of evaluating an organization's management so that improvements can be made, resulting in reduced costs and increased profits for the organization.

To assist in conducting an effective management audit, a management audit questionnaire is useful. It serves as a guide in seeking answers to pertinent questions. From the explanations set forth for negative answers, the real problems can be defined, and appropriate recommendations for their solution can be made. Hence, the questionnaire not only serves as a starting point for a management audit, but it also is of considerable assistance in checking back later when the management auditors define problem areas that require solution. From this latter view, the questionnaire is an important part of the documentation for a management audit.

II

MANAGEMENT AUDITING

of
Financially
Oriented
Functional Areas

3

Evaluating
Corporate Planning

CORPORATE PLANNING, the first of many functional areas to be examined in detail in this text, is the focal point of any management audit questionnaire. In essence, the purpose of corporate planning is to formulate small-, medium-, and large-scale projects that will enable the company to achieve its goals and objectives; decide how to implement these projects in terms of men, materials, machines (including plant facilities), money, and management (5 M's); and decide when to perform them in terms of short-, intermediate-, and long-range plans. Important relationships and feedback exist among these three planning states. Since these relationships are complex, it is extremely important that the management audit questionnaire take a highly systematic and analytic approach to the corporate planning area.

The corporate planning management audit questionnaire is divided into four major secitons:

    I. Overview and Objectives
    II. Plans
    III. Strategies and Programs
    IV. Policies, Procedures, and Standards

After the corporate planning management audit questionnaire is presented (see Figure 3-1), a brief background on the XYZ Company—the text's master case study—is set forth. Two sample applications are demonstrated for this company. In each one, the real problem is defined by utilizing the management audit questionnaire, and appropriate recommendations are enumerated to overcome the problem. Specifically, these applications center on company objectives and strategies.

(text continues on page 45)

Figure 3-1. Management Audit Questionnaire: Corporate Planning.

	YES*	NO†	N.A.‡

I. a. OVERVIEW

    A. External Environmental Considerations:

      1. Does the company, including its management, have a good public image? ___ ___ ___

      2. Is the company a leader in its industry? ___ ___ ___

      3. Is there competition in its industry? ___ ___ ___

      4. Are there specific market segments to which the company caters? ___ ___ ___

      5. Is the company highly regarded in its major markets? ___ ___ ___

      6. Are the company's products preferred by its customers? ___ ___ ___

      7. Is the company favored because of its location? ___ ___ ___

      8. Does the company comply with government regulations? ___ ___ ___

      9. Does the company respond quickly to government regulations? ___ ___ ___

    B. Internal Environmental Considerations:

      1. Are stockholders favorably disposed toward the company? ___ ___ ___

      2. Does the company have an effective board of directors? ___ ___ ___

      3. Does the company have an effective top management team? ___ ___ ___

      4. Does the company have effective lower-level and middle-level managers? ___ ___ ___

      5. Does management stress the need for good financial health? ___ ___ ___

      6. Does management stress the need for providing fast customer service? ___ ___ ___

      7. Does management require that the latest technology be used in its manufacturing operations? ___ ___ ___

      8. Does the information system provide timely management information? ___ ___ ___

*Indicates a favorable condition.
†Indicates a condition that needs to be explained (in writing).
‡Not applicable.

	YES	NO	N.A.

9. Does the company enjoy unique cost advantages?

10. Is management's attitude toward employees positive?

11. Is the "management by exception" principle employed?

I. b. OBJECTIVES

A. General Considerations:

1. Are company objectives developed by the board of directors and top management?

2. Has management communicated company objectives that are clear and understandable to company personnel?

3. Does management see to it that company objectives are compatible with:
   a. plans?
   b. strategies?
   c. programs?
   d. policies?
   e. procedures?
   f. standards?

4. Are company objectives stated in specific, measurable terms?

5. Are company objectives stated in writing?

B. Characteristics of Objectives:

1. Are company objectives capable of being measured?

2. Is there a hierarchy of company objectives that states:
   a. overall objectives?
   b. major objectives?
   c. intermediate objectives?
   d. minor objectives?
   e. individual objectives?

3. Is there a network of company objectives that relates one functional area to another?

4. Does the company have a specific set of objectives for the corporate planning group?

	YES	NO	N.A.

5. Does the company have objectives for each functional area:
   a. accounting and finance?
   b. marketing, including physical distribution?
   c. research & development and engineering?
   d. manufacturing, including inventory and purchasing?
   e. personnel?
   f. computer operations?

C. Overall Organization Objectives:
   1. Does the company have an economic service objective, that is, does the company place its products and/or services for customers first, over profits?
   2. Are the overall company objectives broadly stated (rather than so narrowly that they will have to be changed frequently)?
   3. Do company objectives include provision for:
      a. growth?
      b. survival?
   4. Does management recognize personal objectives of its work force?
   5. Is there a recognition of government and societal objectives, such as reducing pollution and hiring minority groups?

D. Specific Organization Objectives:
   1. Are specific objectives stated on a *flexible* budgeting basis?
   2. Are there managerial productivity factors for measuring company efficiency?
   3. Are objectives that can be measured by "how much" stated in quantitative terms?
   4. Are objectives that can be gauged by "how well" stated in qualitative terms?

E. Management Concern for Objectives:
   1. Does management require that the company be managed by objectives?

	YES	NO	N.A.

2. Do managers assist their superiors in setting objectives? ___ ___ ___

3. Are specific action plans developed for each manager and subordinates? ___ ___ ___

4. Are periodic reviews conducted to determine if stated objectives have been accomplished? ___ ___ ___

5. Is there an appraisal of annual performance for management and non-management personnel? ___ ___ ___

II. a. LONG-RANGE PLANS

A. General Considerations:

1. Are long-range plans subordinated to company objectives? ___ ___ ___

2. Are long-range plans approved and backed by:
   a. the board of directors? ___ ___ ___
   b. top management? ___ ___ ___

3. Are the following subordinated to long-range plans:
   a. strategies? ___ ___ ___
   b. programs? ___ ___ ___
   c. policies? ___ ___ ___

4. Are the following subordinated to long-range plans:
   a. medium-range plans? ___ ___ ___
   b. short-range plans? ___ ___ ___

5. Are long-range plans an integral part of company functions, including:
   a. accounting and finance? ___ ___ ___
   b. marketing, including physical distribution? ___ ___ ___
   c. research & development and engineering? ___ ___ ___
   d. manufacturing, including inventory and purchasing? ___ ___ ___
   e. personnel? ___ ___ ___
   f. computer operations? ___ ___ ___

6. Are long-range plans challenging enough to motivate company personnel? ___ ___ ___

7. Is there measurement of management performance against long-range plans? ___ ___ ___

8. Do specific long-range plans provide for results that can be measured? ___ ___ ___

YES   NO   N.A.

9. Are long-range plans acceptable to:
   a. stockholders? ___ ___ ___
   b. board of directors? ___ ___ ___
   c. top management? ___ ___ ___
   d. middle management? ___ ___ ___
   e. lower management? ___ ___ ___
10. Do the appropriate management levels understand and accept the long-range plans? ___ ___ ___
11. Are managerial efforts directed toward accomplishing these plans? ___ ___ ___
12. Are long-range plans reviewed periodically and kept current? ___ ___ ___
13. Are long-range plans sufficiently flexible to accommodate changing conditions? ___ ___ ___
14. Is there an official planning committee to develop long-range plans? ___ ___ ___
15. Are mathematical and/or statistical techniques used in long-range planning? ___ ___ ___
16. Have forecasts been sufficiently accurate to develop long-range plans? ___ ___ ___
17. Is the "management by exception" principle an integral part of long-range planning? ___ ___ ___

II. b. SHORT- OR MEDIUM- RANGE PLANS

A. General Considerations:

1. Are short- or medium-range plans compatible with long-range plans? ___ ___ ___
2. Are short- or medium-range plans approved and backed by top management? ___ ___ ___
3. Are short- or medium-range plans integrated with company:
   a. objectives? ___ ___ ___
   b. strategies? ___ ___ ___
   c. programs? ___ ___ ___
   d. policies? ___ ___ ___
   e. procedures? ___ ___ ___
   f. standards? ___ ___ ___
4. Are short- or medium-range plans, including flexible budgets, an integral part of:
   a. accounting and finance? ___ ___ ___

	YES	NO	N.A.
b. marketing, including physical distribution?	—	—	—
c. research & development and engineering?	—	—	—
d. manufacturing, including inventory and purchasing?	—	—	—
e. personnel?	—	—	—
f. computer operations?	—	—	—
5. Are short- or medium-range plans coordinated between the company's functions, enumerated in (4) above?	—	—	—
6. Are short- or medium-range plans, including flexible budgets, fully understood by:			
a. top management?	—	—	—
b. middle management?	—	—	—
c. lower management?	—	—	—
7. Are short- or medium-range plans reviewed periodically, say monthly, and kept current?	—	—	—
8. Are alternative short- or medium-range plans created in case of unexpected changes in the:			
a. external environment?	—	—	—
b. internal environment?	—	—	—
9. Have past short- or medium-range plans generally been achieved?	—	—	—
10. Are short- or medium-range management reports tailored to meet the needs of:			
a. management?	—	—	—
b. the organization?	—	—	—
c. operating personnel?	—	—	—
11. Are present short- or medium-range plans realistic?	—	—	—
12. Is the "management by exception" principle an integral part of short- or medium-range planning?	—	—	—

III. a. STRATEGIES

A. Overall Considerations:

	YES	NO	N.A.
1. Are strategies compatible with company objectives?	—	—	—
2. Are strategies approved and backed by top management?	—	—	—

	YES	NO	N.A.
3. Do personnel understand the relationship of company objectives to strategies?	___	___	___
4. Are company strategies understood by company personnel?	___	___	___
5. Are company strategies integrated with:			
a. programs?	___	___	___
b. policies?	___	___	___
c. procedures?	___	___	___
d. standards?	___	___	___
6. Are strategies an integral part of:			
a. long-range plans?	___	___	___
b. medium-range plans?	___	___	___
c. short-range plans?	___	___	___

B. Specific Considerations:

	YES	NO	N.A.
1. Are strategies reviewed periodically to reflect specific:			
a. social trends?	___	___	___
b. social needs?	___	___	___
c. technological changes?	___	___	___
2. Are specific strategies an essential part of strategic planning?	___	___	___
3. Are specific strategies incorporated into the company's functional areas where applicable?	___	___	___

III. b. PROGRAMS

A. Overall Considerations:

	YES	NO	N.A.
1. Are programs planned to meet company objectives?	___	___	___
2. Are programs approved and backed by top management?	___	___	___
3. Do personnel understand the relationship of company objectives to programs?	___	___	___
4. Are programs integrated with:			
a. strategies?	___	___	___
b. policies?	___	___	___
c. procedures?	___	___	___
d. standards?	___	___	___
5. Are programs an integral part of:			
a. long-range plans?	___	___	___
b. medium-range plans?	___	___	___
c. short-range plans?	___	___	___

	YES	NO	N.A.

B. Specific Considerations:

1. Are programs reviewed frequently and brought up to date?
2. Are programs sufficiently flexible to accommodate changing conditions?
3. Are programs supported by capital or operating budgets?
4. Is there a hierarchy of derivative subprograms that are in agreement with the overall program?
5. Are programs terminated when they have met their stated purpose?

IV. a. POLICIES

A. Overall Considerations:

1. Does the company have written policies that are in harmony with its objectives?
2. Are policies approved and backed by management?
3. Is there a stated policy process that includes:
   a. formulation?
   b. dissemination?
   c. education?
   d. acceptance?
   e. application?
   f. interpretation?
   g. control?
4. Have policies been developed for all of the company's functional areas?
5. Are policies reviewed periodically in order to reflect changed conditions?
6. Are policies understood and practiced by company personnel?

B. Specific Considerations:

1. Does each company policy contain:
   a. a basic principle?
   b. a rule of action (a restrictive statement of this principle for a given situation)?
2. Is each policy:
   a. based on organization objectives?
   b. capable of relating functions, physical factors, and company personnel?

                                                    YES   NO   N.A.

    c. in conformity with ethical busi-
       ness standards?   ____   ____   ____

    d. capable of being understood and
       stated in writing?   ____   ____   ____

    e. stable with flexibility for changing
       conditions?   ____   ____   ____

    f. sufficiently comprehensive in
       scope?   ____   ____   ____

    g. complementary to coordinate pol-
       icies?   ____   ____   ____

    h. supplementary to superior poli-
       cies?   ____   ____   ____

IV. b. PROCEDURES

A. Overall Considerations:

1. Do procedures assist in fulfilling specific company objectives?   ____   ____   ____

2. Are procedures approved and backed by management?   ____   ____   ____

3. Do personnel at all levels understand how to use company procedures?   ____   ____   ____

4. Are procedures written and self-explanatory?   ____   ____   ____

5. Are procedures operating effectively (that is, are they fulfilling the purpose for which they were designed)?   ____   ____   ____

6. Are procedures flexible to accommodate changing conditions?   ____   ____   ____

B. Specific Considerations:

1. Do detailed procedures establish:
    a. task(s) to be performed?   ____   ____   ____
    b. responsibilities of individuals involved?   ____   ____   ____
    c. departmental interfaces?   ____   ____   ____

2. Do detailed procedures:
    a. make a contribution to the flow of work?   ____   ____   ____
    b. perform the task(s) as quickly as possible?   ____   ____   ____
    c. perform the task(s) in an economical manner?   ____   ____   ____
    d. relieve the manager of much of the detail in directing subordinates?   ____   ____   ____
    e. aid in placing responsibility so that accountability can be established?   ____   ____   ____
    f. allow for exceptions from planned performance to be highlighted?   ____   ____   ____

	YES	NO	N.A.

IV. c. STANDARDS

   A. Overall Considerations:

      1. Do standards assist in measuring the accomplishment of specific company objectives? ___ ___ ___

      2. Are standards approved and backed by management? ___ ___ ___

      3. Do company personnel understand how to measure actual results against standards? ___ ___ ___

      4. Are standards written and self-explanatory? ___ ___ ___

      5. Are company standards categorized as to:

         a. quantity? ___ ___ ___

         b. time? ___ ___ ___

         c. cost? ___ ___ ___

         d. quality? ___ ___ ___

   B. Specific Considerations:

      1. Are specific *quantitative* standards of time and cost used as guidelines for measuring future performance? ___ ___ ___

      2. Are specific *qualitative* standards used as guidelines for measuring future performance? ___ ___ ___

      3. Do specific standards allow for "management by exception" to be practiced? ___ ___ ___

COMMENTS ON THE CORPORATE PLANNING QUESTIONNAIRE

Before examining the corporate planning management audit questionnaire in detail, it would be well to review some general comments about the questionnaire. Basically, the management audit questionnaire is a managerial tool designed to identify specific problem areas. It does not provide answers to problems, but rather is an approach to evaluating managerial (and operational) effectiveness or lack thereof. Within the questionnaire, a yes answer indicates that there is no need for an explanation since the area investigated is functioning in an acceptable manner. In contrast, a no answer must be explained in writing, since it signals problems or deficiencies. An "N.A." (not applicable) answer denotes that the question should be ignored in the management audit.

Overview and Objectives

Section I of the corporate planning questionnaire examines the organization's overall effectiveness and organization objectives. Subsection I.a. centers on external and internal environmental factors affecting corporate planning. If most or all questions are answered in the affirmative, the company would seem to be responsive to changing conditions, and its chances for growth and survival are good in the long run. On the other hand, if many questions are answered no, it would appear that the company is non-progressive. Suceeding sections of the management audit questionnaire would also bring this unfavorable condition to light.

One of the most important management principles contained in this part of the questionnaire and its succeeding parts is *management by exception*. Fundamentally, only extraordinary events—favorable or unfavorable—are brought to the attention of those responsible and accountable for results. Often, exceptions to established plans, procedures, or standards are referred to the next higher level of command. Thus, a manager gives attention only to those matters that deviate from an established level and thereby require some type of action. Also, this principle ensures that normal events are processed without management's attention.

Subsection I.b. examines various aspects of organization objectives. Overall and specific objectives, as well as management's concern for objectives, are evaluated. The purpose of this section is to determine the degree of concern for organization objectives and their effectiveness in coordinating strategies, programs, policies, procedures, and standards. A predominance of yes answers indicates that the company makes good use of organization objectives, while a series of no answers is indicative of poor management.

An important way of measuring the accomplishment of objectives is through the use of *flexible budgets*. Flexible budgeting involves determining revenue and cost values at stated levels of produciton, say, 70 percent, 75 percent, or 80 percent. When comparing actual values to budgeted values for the current month or period, the values for the closest production level are used. In this manner, there is a meaningful comparison of actual revenue and cost values so that the manager can be held accountable for meeting predetermined yet realistic budget objectives.

Just as flexible budgeting can be utilized in measuring performance, so can managerial productivity factors. From a broad viewpoint, productivity factors relate to producing more with the same amount of effort. It is a matter of getting employees to work more efficiently, not of making them work longer or harder. More specifically, managerial productivity factors relate to better planning, improved technology, employment of improved production techniques, greater efficiency of equipment, and more ingenuity. In short, they result from better exercise of the functions of management.

Plans

Section II.a. of the corporate planning management audit questionnaire contains questions on long-range planning. These overview questions explore not only long-range plans, but also an organization's major functional areas.

Because of the importance of long-range plans for the organization's functional areas, they are explored in detail in the forthcoming chapters. More specifically, subsections on long-range plans are set forth as follows:

Accounting and finance overview—Chapter 4
    Accounting
    Finance
Marketing overview—Chapter 5
    Sales
    Market research
    Advertising
    Physical distribution
Research & development and engineering overview—Chapter 6
    Research & development
    Engineering
Manufacturing overview—Chapter 7
    Production planning
    Production
    Inventory
    Purchasing
Personnel overview—Chapter 8
    Manpower planning
    Industrial relations

For the most part, these subsections on long-range plans constitute one-fifth of the management audit questionnaire for each functional area.

When the time frame for the questions asked in the first subsection on long-range plans is narrowed, the accent is on short- to medium-range plans. Whereas the long-range planning questions center on comprehensive needs of the organization five years and beyond, the short-range subsection of the questionnaire is concerned with the effectiveness of plans for the coming year as well as daily, weekly, monthly, or other relatively short-time periods. In effect, the short-range planning subsections focus on the effective implementation of organization plans on a day-by-day basis. On the other hand, if the time frame is extended beyond one year and up to five years, the focus is on medium-range planning. General considerations for both short- and medium-range corporate planning are covered by Section II.b. of the corporate planning questionnaire. Additionally, one-fifth of the management audit questionnaire for each of the functional areas set forth above centers on short- or medium-range plans.

Strategies and Programs

Section III of the corporate planning management audit questionnaire focuses on evaluating the effectiveness of strategies and programs. Subsection III.a. serves to assess how able the firm is to develop innovative strategies, both general and specific—that is, how effectively the organization relates to social trends and technological changes. Fundamentally, strategies relate to the determination of long-range goals and objectives of an enterprise and the adaption of courses of action and the allocation of resources necessary to carry out these goals. Affirmative answers denote a high degree of strategic planning—the desired direction for any organization.

Subsection III.b.—*Programs*—is logically related to strategies, since major projects are undertaken to capitalize on social and technological changes taking place. Product development programs based on new technology, large capital expansion programs to build new plants, and long-range programs to hire the hard-core unemployed are examples. Overall, this section determines how effective management is in developing organization programs that are in tune with the social trends and technological changes.

Policies, Procedures, and Standards

In the final section of the corporate planning management audit questionnaire, the main thrust is on policies, procedures, and standards. To understand the rationale for this inclusion, it should be noted that organization plans based on appropriate programs and strategies need to be supplemented with policies, that is, guiding principles of operation to achieve organization objectives. In a similar manner, organization plans must be supplemented with detailed specifications on how they operate. Hence, the need for procedures is apparent. Also, there is need to compare the actual results with the original plans. Standards are usable as selected criteria against which actual results can be measured to evaluate performance. Overall, corporate planning at the highest level—objectives and plans—must be specified in terms of strategies and programs, which, in turn, must be broken down for daily operations in the form of policies, procedures, and standards.

Subsection IV.a. of the corporate planning questionnaire examines the general and specific company policies that help an organization in following a planned course of action to reach its objectives. Properly communicated policies provide a uniform means of coordinating and accomplishing tasks in a consistent and economical manner. Policies must be complied with at all times until valid reasons indicate a change. Also, the policies should complement one another. For example, a purchasing policy should complement a manufacturing policy so that the two functions can cooperate effectively. Likewise, they should be supplementary; that is, overall, policies should be broken down into supportive policies. Generally, most organizations will score favorably on this section, even if they scored fair or poorly on the earlier sections.

The questions in subsection IV.b consider the extent to which organization procedures are meeting current requirements and their degree of operating effectiveness and efficiency. Since procedures are designed to meet desired results, they are an important and integral part of setting company standards. Questions on standards are covered in the final subsection. Whether dealing with procedures or standards, too many negative answers can mean that activities under the control of operational managers are not being performed in an optimum manner.

MASTER CASE STUDY—XYZ COMPANY

The application of the management audit questionnaire to a typical company—the XYZ Company—illustrates how the questionnaire can be used not only to identify organizational problems but also to develop tentative solutions to overcome these problems. This problem-solving process results in specific recommendations to management that are compatible with the organization's stated objectives.

As will be demonstrated throughout the forthcoming case studies of the XYZ Company, there are managerial problems occurring at various levels. Because of the diversity of problems encountered, it is recommended that the consultant start with the highest-level executive whose area is under investigation, that is, a vice president. In this manner, a broad perspective of the problem area can be gained before looking at its detailed aspects at a lower level. This orientation allows the consultant not only to get a broad view of the problem, but also to offer recommendations that optimize results for the entire firm, not only for some part of it. On the other hand, if it is obvious to the consultant that the problem is narrow in scope and should be treated as such, the consultant need not start at the highest level but should study the problem and offer recommendations at the level being studied.

The XYZ Company is a small- to medium-size firm engaged in the manufacture and distribution of low-priced consumer products. Current sales are $80 million per year and projected to be over $110 million in less than five years. Growth is projected from the existing line, which currently numbers about 40 products. These products are classified into six basic lines. Variations of these products are for specific retailers whose requirements differ because of the markets they serve. For extremely large orders, products are shipped directly from the firm's manufacturing plants. These orders account for about 25 percent of total sales. For the bulk of the sales volume, merchandise is shipped from the firm's warehouses to retailers.

Corporate headquarters of the XYZ Company is located in a large midwestern city, while its manufacturing plants and distribution centers are located throughout the country. There are four manufacturing plants and twelve distribution centers. Each manufacturing plant has an attached warehouse. The present employment level is 2,500 employees, which is expected to grow at a 1 percent rate over the next few years.

The company is organized around the major functions set forth previously (see Chapter 1): accounting and finance, marketing, research & development and engineering, manufacturing, and personnel. In addition to vice presidents for each of these areas, there is a vice president in charge of the company's computerized information system. These six vice presidents report to the executive vice president, who, in turn, reports to the president. The president (chief executive officer) is assisted by a corporate planning staff. The function of this group is to formulate challenging short- to long-range plans that meet the mandates of the board of directors. This group is very influential and responsible for developing important strategies, programs, and appropriate policies that are capable of meeting organization objectives.

This brief background on the XYZ Company serves to place selected corporate planning problems in their proper perspective as they are evaluated within the framework of a management audit questionnaire. Later in the text, case studies on the XYZ Company will focus on its major functional areas.

APPLICATION OF THE MANAGEMENT AUDIT QUESTIONNAIRE TO COMPANY OBJECTIVES

At a recent meeting of the XYZ Company's top management team (president, executive vice president, and six vice presidents), one item, namely, defining company objectives by the president for the new vice president of research & development and engineering, resulted in a stormy meeting. The new vice president, who had been on the job only one month and came from outside the company, was not satisfied with the response by the president. The vice president suggested that the item be tabled for their next monthly meeting, at which time the president would give a more definite answer.

The statement on objectives that caused a lot of controversy was the following:

> The basic objective of the XYZ Company is to operate a vigorous, growing, and diversified business in the balanced interest of its stockholders, customers, employees, suppliers, and the economy at large by generating optimum profits so as to develop a sound financial position which will allow payment of dividends to stockholders sufficient to warrant their continued investment in the company and, at the same time, sufficient for retention of funds in the business to assure growth.

It should be noted that this statement was approved by the board of directors many years ago and has served as a guiding light for the company over the years.

The main thrust of the new vice president's comments was summarized by this statement: "While generalized objectives can sometimes have an inspirational value, they are usually a detriment to performance, since they forestall the development of specific and useful objectives. In addition, managers can avoid performance responsibility by taking advantage of semantic confusion." In essence, no one within or outside the organization can tell precisely if vague objectives are being met. He concluded by stating, "Without measurable limits, objectives are useless."

The president, to get himself "off the hook," engaged the services of a consultant who is presently on the company's board of directors. Because of the president's request that he do a comprehensive study of the company's objectives, the consultant decided to use the corporate planning management audit questionnaire, in particular, the subsection on objectives. His evaluation is shown in Figure 3-2.

Before completing the questionnaire, the consultant spent one afternoon interviewing the new vice president in charge of research & development and engineering. An intensive discussion with the vice president uncovered the fact that the lack of clearly stated, measurable objectives had been the reason for his departure from another firm. In effect, he did not want this unfortunate situation to occur again. In a follow-up interview, the vice president reiterated his criticism of generalized objectives. Additionally, he commented on the higher-than-normal turnover of engineers, which he discovered recently. Thus, the vice president felt that the consultant should go beyond the initial problem and offer additional recommendations for study by the board of directors.

Answers to the first group of questions by the consultant indicate that items 2 and 4 are negative. Not only are company objectives not clear and understandable to company personnel, but also they are not stated in spe-

Figure 3-2. XYZ Company evaluation of company objectives.

	YES	NO	N.A.
I. b. OBJECTIVES			
A. General Considerations:			
1. Are company objectives developed by the board of directors and top management?	X		
2. Has management communicated company objectives that are clear and understandable to company personnel?		X	
3. Does management see to it that company objectives are compatible with:			
a. plans?	X		
b. strategies?	X		
c. programs?	X		
d. policies?	X		
e. procedures?	X		
f. standards?	X		
4. Are company objectives stated in specific, measurable terms?		X	
5. Are company objectives stated in writing?	X		
B. Characteristics of Objectives:			
1. Are company objectives capable of being measured?		X	
2. Is there a hierarchy of company objectives that states:			
a. overall objectives?	X		
b. major objectives?	X		
c. intermediate objectives?	X		
d. minor objectives?	X		
e. individual objectives?	X		
3. Is there a network of company objectives that relates one functional area to another?	X		
4. Does the company have a specific set of objectives for the corporate planning group?	X		
5. Does the company have objectives for each functional area:			
a. accounting and finance?	X		
b. marketing, including physical distribution?	X		
c. research & development and engineering?	X		
d. manufacturing, including inventory and purchasing?	X		
e. personnel?	X		
f. computer operations?	X		

Questionnaire Comments (Negative Answers):

A. General Considerations:

Question 2   Company objectives are far from clear to its executives, not to mention personnel below them.

Question 4   Company objectives are stated in general terms that are too vague for holding managers responsible and accountable.

B. Characteristics of Objectives:

Question 1   Company objectives are capable of being measured only in general terms and not in precise ones.

---

cific, measurable terms. The same fact is brought out in the second group of questions, that is, company objectives are not capable of being measured.

Recommendations to Improve Company Objectives

Although sections of the corporate planning questionnaire were investigated by the consultant, the main thrust of the evaluation is that company objectives are too vague for holding management responsible and accountable for its actions. In view of this fact, the following recommendations are in order to change the overly general company objectives into more workable and realizable ones.

The consultant recommended that the generalized objective given above for "generating optimum profits" be changed to:

The company shall seek to earn a rate of return on invested capital each year that is at least equal to the average rate of return for its five competitors having annual sales closest to those of the company.

Similarly, "to develop a sound financial position" is to be reworded as:

The company shall develop a sound financial position, which shall be measured by its maintaining a current assets to current liabilities ratio of at least two-to-one and a long-term debt to capital ratio of not more than one to one.

Also, the consultant recommended that once specific, measurable objectives are established and agreed upon by the top management team, they be made an integral part of the company's information system. The organization can add to the effectiveness of the management system by making the objectives attainable. Actual performance can be reported in relation to the measures and target values that have been set in the objectives. The management planning and control functions can be served with increased usefulness because objectives and results are expressed in the same terms.

Additionally, the consultant recommended that company objectives be broadened to include more than those discussed above. One recommended new objective relates to stabilizing employment:

> The company shall seek to stabilize employment. Specifically, the overall turnover ratio for employees each year should be lower than the average personnel turnover rate for its five competitors having a total number of employees closest to that of the company.

Environmental issues, such as pollution control and urban development, and social issues, such as hiring the hard-core unemployed and financing new undertakings for minority groups, were also recommended to be included as an integral part of organization objectives.

Overall, the consultant's recommendations need to be discussed at the next monthly meeting. Ultimately, the net result should be a feasible set of company objectives that can be used from the highest management level to the lowest level.

Application of the Management Audit Questionnaire to Company Strategies

During a subsequent monthly meeting of the XYZ Company's top management team, the vice president of research and development and engineering asked the executive vice president what are the company's long-range strategies. The executive stated that the company's long-range strategies refer to the broad, overall deployment of the firm's resources to achieve organization objectives, or to the determination of the firm's basic long-term goals and objectives and the adoption of courses of action and the allocation of resources necessary to carry out these goals.

After a rather lengthy exchange of ideas on the subject, the vice president of research and development and engineering was not satisfied with the generalized statement on strategies. What he wanted to hear from the executive vice president was a definitive statement on what constitutes the specific strategies of the XYZ Company. Because they were not stated in sufficient detail but only in general terms, the vice president asked that this item be tabled for the next meeting. At that time, a more detailed statement could be set forth as to the specific strategies for the XYZ Company.

Due to the importance of the question posed, the executive vice president approached the same member of the board who resolved the prior problem. The consultant felt that a logical starting point for assuring that all facets of the problem are scrutinized was to utilize a portion of the corporate planning management audit questionnaire. As illustrated in Figure 3-3, several questions have been answered in the negative.

The basis for the consultant's several negative answers in the questionnaire was the interviews with the executive vice president and the six vice presidents. Specifically, the strategies set forth by the executive vice president were used by the consultant as the basis for discussion with the vice presidents. In the interviewing process, the consultant got the distinct impression that the changing needs of people were understood only in general terms and not in specific terms, except for the research and development and engineering vice president. Thus, the general comments by these high-level executives account for the large number of negative answers in Figure 3-3.

In the first subsection on overall consideration of strategies, questions 3 through 5 have been answered with no. Like the vice president of research and development and engineering, company personnel do not understand the relationship of company objectives to strategies, nor are company strategies themselves understood by company personnel or integrated with programs, policies, procedures, and standards. In addition, all three questions in the next subsection have been answered in the negative, since strategies are not specifically related to social trends and needs, technological changes, planning, and the company's functional areas.

Recommendations to Improve Company Strategies

On the basis of the foregoing answers to the management audit questionnaire, the consultant concluded that company strategies have failed to take into account certain critical items. For one, corporate strategies are drastically affected by accelerating technological advances. The consultant underscored this point with the following statement to the executive vice president: "The direction of technology and organization determines the shape of economic society. Consider the effect of microelectronics on computer systems, containerization on transportation systems, and computerization on office systems. In essence, accelerated technological obsolescence of entire fields of well-established products and services is proceeding daily and has a marked impact on corporate strategies." Because of these and other factors operating within the business environment, the consultant recommended that the XYZ Company adopt a long-term approach to its corporate planning strategy—from the general to the specific. For example, instead of talking about overall strategies to cope with changes occurring on the production floor, the company should focus on specific strategies to cut production

Figure 3-3. XYZ Company evaluation of company strategies.

	YES	NO	N.A.
III. a. STRATEGIES			
A. Overall Considerations:			
1. Are strategies compatible with company objectives?	X		
2. Are strategies approved and backed by top management?	X		
3. Do personnel understand the relationship of company objectives to strategies?		X	
4. Are company strategies understood by company personnel?		X	
5. Are company strategies integrated with:			
a. programs?		X	
b. policies?		X	
c. procedures?		X	
d. standards?		X	
6. Are strategies an integral part of:			
a. long-range plans?	X		
b. medium-range plans?	X		
c. short-range plans?	X		
B. Specific Considerations:			
1. Are strategies reviewed periodically to reflect specific:			
a. social trends?		X	
b. social needs?		X	
c. technological changes?		X	
2. Are specific strategies an essential part of strategic planning?		X	
3. Are specific strategies incorporated into the company's functional areas where applicable?		X	

Questionnaire Comments (Negative Answers):

A. Overall Considerations:

Question 3   The vice president of research & development and engineering feels that company objectives and strategies are related in general terms only and not in specific terms.

Question 4   Because company strategies are stated in general terms, they are not thoroughly understood.

Question 5   Due to the generality of strategies, they are not fully integrated in specific details with programs, policies, procedures, and standards.

B. Specific Considerations:

Question 1   Strategies are reviewed periodically, but only in general terms. Thus, specific items, such as social trends and needs plus technological changes, are not reviewed.

Question 2   Because specific strategies are not set forth, they are not a part of strategic planning.

Question 3   Because specific strategies are not set forth, they are not incorporated into the company's functional areas where applicable.

---

costs, such as the employment of mechanical robots and automatic processes under computer control.

A viable corporate strategy, the consultant noted, must be guided by the changing needs of people. Such an orientation is a key to business success. Social needs express themselves in many ways, such as increasing demands for leisure time, concern about air and water pollution, and the socialization of medical care. An understanding of the XYZ Company's strategies relative to social trends is unquestionably an important factor in developing well-conceived long-range plans. Thus, the consultant recommended that the top management team discuss these social trends and needs at its next meeting.

As the consultant remarked to the executive vice president, by constructively integrating knowledge about technology and social changes with the organization's strategies, the company can better formulate programs that embrace new products, improved technology, enlarged markets, higher earnings, and increased rates of growth. Similarly, he noted that corporate strategies must be dynamic enough to expand traditional boundaries, yet flexible enough to withstand the unexpected. Those strategies that are rooted too deeply in the products and social conditions of today will not be viable in the context of the fast-changing pattern imposed by our technological capabilities. Overall, for the XYZ Company to accommodate these coming changes within its strategies, its objectives must be comprehensive. Otherwise, the consultant stated, the company will find itself in the unfortunate position of missing new and emerging markets.

The recommendations to the executive vice president were somewhat open-ended. The rationale is that the consultant's recommendations will serve as a springboard for discussion by the top management team at the next meeting, which he plans to attend. In essence, the consultant feels that specific strategies must be developed and agreed upon by these top-level executives, or they will not have any real meaning. For this reason, his final recommendations are being held in abeyance and will be enumerated at the proper time during the meeting to give direction to management's thinking.

SUMMARY

Due to the comprehensive nature of corporate planning, this initial part of the management audit questionnaire was divided into the following sections: I. Overview and Objectives, II. Plans, III. Strategies and Programs, and IV. Policies, Procedures, and Standards. This breakdown allows for pinpointing managerial (and operational) deficiencies in planning not only at the top and middle levels of an organization, but also at the lower levels. As explained in the chapter, strategies, programs, policies, procedures, and standards represent the various levels of plans, which must be in conformity with organization objectives.

As the two case studies of the XYZ Company illustrated, the management audit questionnaire provides a means for pinpointing the real problem and is helpful as a starting point in making appropriate recommendations.

4

Evaluating Accounting and Finance

THE ACCOUNTING AND FINANCE PART of the management audit questionnaire is an integral part of a comprehensive evaluation of the financially oriented functional areas. The functions of accounting are evaluated as they relate to recording, classifying, and summarizing transactions and events that are, in part at least, of a financial character, and interpreting managerial results thereof. Of equal importance are questions referring to a periodic balance sheet and income statement as well as comparable statements that are used for evaluation from a management viewpoint.

Comparable types of questions are used in the questionnaire for the finance function. Without the infusion of capital resources when needed, management cannot fulfill its goals and objectives. For this reason, the finance subsystem is related directly to the other subsystems. Although these relationships may not be obvious, they are a viable force in an organization. In essence, evaluation of an organization's finance area is extremely important for relating financial management criteria to established objectives.

The major sections of the accounting and finance part of the management audit questionnaire (see Figure 4-1) include the following:

    I. Accounting and Finance Overview
   II. Accounting
  III. Finance

The various subsections of the foregoing breakdown are not only comprehensive but also adaptable to most situations. This should be apparent in the sample applications presented for the XYZ Company, namely, cost and financial controls.

(text continues on page 73)

**Figure 4-1. Management Audit Questionnaire:
Accounting and Finance.**

	YES	NO	N.A.

I. ACCOUNTING AND FINANCE OVERVIEW

  A. Long-Range Plans:

    1. Are long-range accounting and finance plans in agreement with:

      a. long-range organization objectives? ____ ____ ____

      b. long-range plans of other functional areas? ____ ____ ____

      c. medium-range accounting and finance plans? ____ ____ ____

      d. short-range accounting and finance plans? ____ ____ ____

    2. Are long-range accounting and finance plans reviewed by:

      a. board of directors? ____ ____ ____

      b. top management? ____ ____ ____

    3. Is there an official planning committee to develop long-range accounting and finance plans? ____ ____ ____

    4. Does accounting and finance management accept and understand these long-range plans? ____ ____ ____

    5. Are accounting and finance management efforts directed toward accomplishing these long-range plans? ____ ____ ____

    6. Is performance against long-range accounting and finance plans measured periodically? ____ ____ ____

    7. Are long-range accounting and finance plans reviewed periodically to stay current? ____ ____ ____

    8. Is the "management by exception" principle an integral part of long-range accounting and finance plans? ____ ____ ____

  B. Short- or Medium-Range Plans:

    1. Are short- or medium-range accounting and finance plans in agreement with:

      a. short- or medium-range organization objectives? ____ ____ ____

      b. short- or medium-range plans of other functional areas? ____ ____ ____

      c. long-range accounting and finance plans? ____ ____ ____

	YES	NO	N.A.

2. Are short- or medium-range accounting plans reviewed by:
   a. top management?
   b. middle management?
   c. lower management?
3. Are there procedures for developing short- or medium-range accounting and finance plans?
4. Does accounting and finance management accept and understand these short- or medium-range plans?
5. Are accounting and finance management efforts directed toward accomplishing short- or medium-range plans?
6. Is performance against short- or medium-range plans measured periodically?
7. Are short- or medium-range accounting and finance plans reviewed periodically to stay current?
8. Is the "management by exception" principle an integral part of short- or medium-range accounting and finance plans?

C. Organization Structure:

1. Is the accounting or finance organization chart compatible with other functional organization charts?
2. Is it clear who is charged with responsibility and who has authority over:
   a. accounting?
   b. finance?
3. Does each person in accounting or finance know his or her job well?
4. Are the superior–subordinate relationships made clear in the accounting or finance departments?
5. Are there adequate job descriptions for each accounting or finance position?
6. Is there a competent employee assigned to each accounting or finance position?
7. Is the level of accounting or finance training adequate for:
   a. management?
   b. employees?

YES   NO   N.A.

8. Can the quality of accounting or finance personnel be assessed for:
   a. management? ____ ____ ____
   b. employees? ____ ____ ____
9. Is the accounting or finance department adequately staffed? ____ ____ ____
10. Are reporting relationships clearly defined and understood by accounting or finance personnel? ____ ____ ____
11. Is accounting or finance management held accountable for its actions? ____ ____ ____
12. Is there provision within the accounting or finance department for periodic review of its organization structure? ____ ____ ____

D. Leadership:

1. Does accounting and finance management work together to provide the company with the right funds at the proper time? ____ ____ ____
2. Does accounting and finance management exert the necessary leadership so that funding is adequate for all of the company's functional areas:
   a. marketing, including physical distribution? ____ ____ ____
   b. research & development and engineering? ____ ____ ____
   c. manufacturing, including inventory and purchasing? ____ ____ ____
   d. personnel? ____ ____ ____
   e. computer operations? ____ ____ ____
3. Is there teamwork between the accounting and finance departments? ____ ____ ____
4. Are accounting and finance personnel involved in decisions relating to their work? ____ ____ ____
5. Does accounting and finance management have confidence and trust in its subordinates? ____ ____ ____
6. Do accounting and finance personnel feel free to disclose to their immediate supervisors problematic operating conditions discovered in the course of their duties? ____ ____ ____

	YES	NO	N.A.

E. Communication:

1. Is there an adequate flow of information between accounting and finance for:
   a. investing excess cash funds?
   b. procuring needed funds?
2. Are peak seasonal requirements for funds communicated to top management for approval?
3. Does accounting and finance management maintain a:
   a. favorable company image in pursuing its financial policies?
   b. good relationship with financial institutions?
   c. high credit rating?
   d. good relationship with its vendors?
4. Do accounting and finance personnel feel free to communicate their ideas and constructive criticisms to their superiors?
5. Do accounting and finance personnel feel free to communicate their job satisfaction needs to their superiors?

F. Control:

1. Is there adequate control over accounting and finance goals so that they are compatible with overall organization objectives?
2. Are effective managerial control methods and techniques used in:
   a. accounting?
   b. finance?
3. Is close managerial control maintained over operational costs?
4. Are predetermined financial accounting data compared to actual results (budget versus actual) on a timely basis?
5. Is corrective action undertaken on a timely basis when significant accounting/financial deviations are detected?

II. ACCOUNTING

A. Long-Range Plans:

1. Is accounting management of sufficient caliber to meet long-range accounting objectives?

	YES	NO	N.A.

2. Have finance plans been made an integral part of long-range accounting plans?

3. If products have been unprofitable, are steps being taken to make them profitable?

4. Are standard operating ratios being employed?

5. Is the chart of accounts designed to plan by area of managerial responsibility and accountability?

6. Is there a formal and effective cost reduction program?

7. Are there procedures for employing management by exception in accounting functions?

B. Short- or Medium-Range Plans:

1. Is accounting management of sufficient caliber to meet short- or medium-range accounting objectives?

2. Are short- or medium-range accounting plans coordinated with finance?

3. Are the balance sheet and income statement prepared?

4. Are flexible budgets stated realistically for comparison with actual results?

5. Are the following types of flexible budgets prepared:
    a. cash?
    b. operating?
    c. capital?
    d. work center?
    e. others, as deemed necessary?

6. Are flexible budgets systematized to handle the myriad data?

7. Are flexible budgets prepared for management on a timely basis?

8. Is the management by exception principle employed for flexible budgets?

9. Are flexible budgets periodically updated to reflect changing conditions?

10. Do accounting plans include an effective cost reduction program?

11. Is cost accounting information meaningful to management?

	YES	NO	N.A.

12. Have breakeven points been calculated for the company's products? — — —

13. Do accounting plans include provision for improving cost methods if they are inadequate or unreliable? — — —

C. Organization Structure:

1. Is the accounting department under the direction of a qualified manager? — — —

2. Is the organization structure compatible with utilizing flexible budgets; that is, can individual managers be held accountable for areas under their control by timely comparisons of actual results to flexible budgeted figures? — — —

3. Can the following accounting reports be prepared easily as a byproduct of the information system:
   a. receivables report? — — —
   b. payables report? — — —
   c. payroll report? — — —
   d. cost report? — — —
   e. financial statements? — — —
   f. tax returns? — — —

4. Are accounting data structured so that information on breakeven data and analysis of the profit–volume relationship can be computed with a minimum of effort? — — —

5. Are accounting data structured so that statistical data on sales and costs can be easily computed? — — —

6. Is the organization structure compatible with accounting by profit centers? — — —

7. Does the organization structure provide for analyzing and reporting cost variances on a timely basis in order to initiate corrective action if necessary? — — —

8. Is the accounting structure flexible enough to accommodate business changes, such as rapid expansion or contraction? — — —

9. Is there adequate internal control, specifically:
   a. internal accounting control (details equal summary)? — — —
   b. internal check (one or more persons checking on each other)? — — —

YES   NO   N.A.

D. Leadership:

1. Is the accounting manager a leader, in the sense that he or she exerts the necessary leadership to accomplish accounting objectives and established accounting deadlines? ___ ___ ___

2. Does the accounting management display leadership qualities by undertaking periodic cost evaluations by:
   a. departments and cost centers? ___ ___ ___
   b. products and services? ___ ___ ___
   c. programs and projects? ___ ___ ___

3. Does accounting management require that budget and actual accounting data be prepared on a flexible basis, that is, does it take into account the economic conditions prevailing for the time period under study? ___ ___ ___

4. Does accounting management utilize efficient management methods and techniques so that information needed for all management levels is available in sufficient time to control the operating environment? ___ ___ ___

5. Does accounting management utilize the feedback concept, i.e., are out-of-control conditions examined for remedial action? ___ ___ ___

6. Is accounting management capable of enacting important accounting policies that are necessary for efficient and economical operations? ___ ___ ___

7. Does accounting recognize that lower-level operating units require different controls than those at the upper levels? ___ ___ ___

E. Communication:

1. Are accounting reports and summaries that are prepared by an information system communicated on a timely basis so that they can affect present and future operations? ___ ___ ___

2. Are appropriate accounting/managerial reports properly communicated to:
   a. the planning group? ___ ___ ___
   b. marketing management? ___ ___ ___
   c. research & development and engineering management? ___ ___ ___
   d. manufacturing management? ___ ___ ___

	YES	NO	N.A.

    e. personnel management?

    f. financial management?

3. Is accounting information accurate before it is transmitted to the appropriate source:

    a. within the organization?

    b. outside the organization?

4. Are cost variances analyzed and forwarded to the appropriate personnel for correction?

5. Is there an adequate system of feedback on exception items?

6. Do accounting employees feel free to discuss accounting problems with their superiors?

F. Control:

    1. Are accounting/management control reports:

        a. timely?

        b. simple to use?

        c. properly designed?

    2. Are budgets stated on a flexible (variable) basis to reflect current conditions?

    3. Are flexible budgets used effectively by managers?

    4. Is the management by exception principle employed for flexible budgets?

    5. Are flexible budgets of the following types prepared:

        a. cash?

        b. operating?

        c. capital?

        d. work center?

        e. others, as deemed necessary?

    6. Do management control center reports provide meaningful operating information to managers?

    7. Do cost accounting reports provide meaningful cost analysis information to managers?

    8. Is intelligent use made of cost data in:

        a. setting sales prices?

        b. valuing inventories?

        c. preparing financial statements?

        d. controlling operations?

        e. determining cost–volume relationships?

	YES	NO	N.A.

9. If products are unprofitable, is this information communicated to the proper authorities?

10. Is control exercised by management over *controllable* costs, such as direct materials and direct labor?

11. Is control exercised by management over *period* costs, such as insurance and personal property taxes?

12. Is there sufficient managerial control over:
   a. accounts receivable?
   b. bad debts?
   c. fixed assets?
   d. other assets?
   e. accounts payable?
   f. other payables?

13. Are there effective internal accounting control (details equal summary) procedures in use?

14. Are there effective internal check (one or more persons checking on each other) procedures in use?

III. FINANCE

A. Long-Range Plans:

1. Is finance management of sufficient caliber to meet long-range finance objectives?

2. Are long-range finance plans compatible with company objectives?

3. Are long-range finance plans coordinated with:
   a. marketing, including physical distribution?
   b. research & development and engineering?
   c. manufacturing, including inventory and purchasing?
   d. accounting?
   e. personnel?

4. Are long-range plans prepared on a formal basis for:
   a. three to five years?
   b. five years?
   c. beyond five years?

	YES	NO	N.A.

5. Are long-range finance plans prepared by areas of managerial responsibility?

6. Are mathematical or statistical models employed to assist in the preparation of long-range finance plans?

7. Are long-range finance reports tailored to meet:
   a. organization needs?
   b. managerial needs?

8. Are long-range finance plans timely?

9. Are alternative finance plans developed for possibly changing conditions?

10. Are the following long-range finance data prepared:
    a. a balance sheet?
    b. an income statement?
    c. a cash flow statement?
    d. a source of funds statement?
    e. an application of funds statement?
    f. return on total assets?
    g. return on stockholder's investment?
    h. weighted cost of capital?

11. If plans are financially undesirable, are there prescribed procedures to develop alternative long-range plans?

12. Are finance plans reviewed by responsible top-level executives for the purpose of developing the best possible ones?

13. Do the company's financial results compare favorably with its industry's:
    a. profits?
    b. return on investment?
    c. inventory turnover?
    d. working capital?

14. Are all of the company's long-range finance plans in writing?

B. Short- or Medium-Range Plans:

1. Is finance management of sufficient caliber to meet short- or medium-range finance objectives?

2. Are short- or medium-range finance plans coordinated with accounting?

3. Is there a written financial plan for next year?

YES   NO   N.A.

4. Is this written financial plan realistic? ___ ___ ___
5. Do short- or medium-range finance plans provide for the company to be in a sound financial position? ___ ___ ___
6. Do short- or medium-range finance plans include a desired level for:
    a. sales? ___ ___ ___
    b. profits? ___ ___ ___
    c. working capital? ___ ___ ___
    d. return on assets? ___ ___ ___
    e. return on investment? ___ ___ ___
    f. cost of capital? ___ ___ ___
    g. growth? ___ ___ ___
7. Is a cash flow forecast prepared? ___ ___ ___
8. Is a source and application of funds statement prepared? ___ ___ ___
9. Are appropriate financial statements prepared to supplement the balance sheet and income statement? ___ ___ ___
10. Do financial plans provide for comparison of actual performance and projected results? ___ ___ ___
11. Are financial plans flexible so as to provide for changing conditions? ___ ___ ___
12. Are mathematical or statistical techniques employed to improve the reliability of short- or medium-range finance plans? ___ ___ ___
13. Are short- or medium-range finance plans prepared on a timely basis? ___ ___ ___

C. Organization Structure:
1. Is the finance department under the direction of a qualified manager? ___ ___ ___
2. Is the finance function integrated with the corporate planning function? ___ ___ ___
3. Are finance procedures an integral part of an information system? ___ ___ ___
4. Is finance organized so that future cash flows indicate:
    a. an excess of funds? ___ ___ ___
    b. a deficiency of funds? ___ ___ ___
    c. peak requirements of funds? ___ ___ ___
5. Is the finance function organized so that short- to long-term funds can be obtained externally with a minimum of time and effort? ___ ___ ___

YES   NO   N.A.

6. Are capital budgeting procedures logically related to the organization structure? —— —— ——
7. Is there adequate internal control over:
   a. application of funds? —— —— ——
   b. source of funds? —— —— ——

D. Leadership:

1. Is the finance department manager a leader, that is, does he or she exert the required leadership to accomplish established finance objectives? —— —— ——
2. Does finance management exert itself in making company personnel at all levels responsible and accountable for a satisfactory return on invested capital? —— —— ——
3. Does finance management practice the cash flow concept to prepare for periods of cash shortages and cash overages? —— —— ——
4. Does finance management exert itself in investing excess cash funds in order to maximize the company's return on total assets? —— —— ——
5. Does finance management play an active role in keeping the following items under control:
   a. inventory? —— —— ——
   b. accounts receivable? —— —— ——
   c. accounts payable? —— —— ——
   d. bad debts? —— —— ——
   e. notes payable? —— —— ——
   f. bonds payable? —— —— ——
6. Do finance personnel feel free to discuss potential problems concerning company assets and liabilities with their superiors? —— —— ——
7. Are finance personnel involved in decisions that are related directly or closely to their work? —— —— ——

E. Communication:

1. Does finance management communicate the most advantageous financing to the planning group for company expansion? —— —— ——

	YES	NO	N.A.

2. Does finance management help in the preparation of short- to long-range plans and possible alternatives to these plans? ___ ___ ___

3. Does finance management communicate to top management its recommendations and suggestions on financial plans, including those that maximize cash flow and reduce taxes? ___ ___ ___

4. Is there adequate information communicated to top management on:
   a. breakeven data? ___ ___ ___
   b. profit–volume relationships? ___ ___ ___

5. Does finance management communicate all relevant information to lower and middle managers as rapidly as possible? ___ ___ ___

6. Does finance management communicate to the appropriate management levels the return on invested capital:
   a. for future acquistions? ___ ___ ___
   b. on present investments? ___ ___ ___

7. Are unfavorable returns on investments and assets communicated to the appropriate management level, including the board of directors? ___ ___ ___

F. Control:

1. Does the treasurer exert sufficient control so that the company maintains a sound financial position? ___ ___ ___

2. Does the treasurer exert sufficient control over cash flow to:
   a. maximize its usage? ___ ___ ___
   b. pay the company's obligations? ___ ___ ___

3. Does the treasurer exert sufficient influence so that company taxes are kept as low as possible? ___ ___ ___

4. Are financial/managerial reports, methods, and techniques used, including:
   a. cash forecasts? ___ ___ ___
   b. balance sheet? ___ ___ ___
   c. income statement? ___ ___ ___
   d. management control center reports? ___ ___ ___
   e. source and application of funds statement? ___ ___ ___
   f. budgets? ___ ___ ___
   g. financial ratios? ___ ___ ___

	YES	NO	N.A.
h. breakeven analysis?	——	——	——
i. return on investment?	——	——	——
j. costing methods?	——	——	——
5. Are financial control reports prepared on a basis that provides for changing conditions?	——	——	——
6. Is there an adequate cash balance to take advantage of discounts offered on purchased items?	——	——	——
7. Is adequate control maintained over discounts offered on purchased items?	——	——	——
8. Are discounted cash flow or similar methods used to evelute capital expenditures?	——	——	——
9. Is the management by exception principle utilized for financial/managerial control reports, methods, and techniques?	——	——	——

COMMENTS ON THE ACCOUNTING AND FINANCE QUESTIONNAIRE

Accounting and Finance Overview

Accounting and finance are an integral part of many other functional areas; that is, information is generated by marketing, manufacturing, personnel, and so on, which then becomes input for accounting and finance activities. This information is processed by accounting and finance to issue timely management and operational reports. In turn, these meaningful reports serve as input for planning and controlling diverse organization activities. Thus, the accounting and finance departments serve as an information processing medium for an organization's functional areas.

An important purpose of the overview section of the accounting and finance management audit questionnaire is to evaluate whether or not the reporting requirements of managers at all levels are being met. A concurrent reason is to evaluate the interface between the two functions and the other functional areas that come into contact with accounting and finance. Thus, this opening section determines the capability of accounting and finance departments to produce managerial and operational information for running an organization in an efficient and economical manner.

Accounting

To ensure proper utilization of accounting information, the first subsection of long-range plans centers on accounting questions that are oriented toward the future. When the time frame is shortened, questions relating to short- or medium-range accounting plans are asked. For the most part, this refers to the adequacy of such accounting items as flexible budgets and cost accounting to meet current managerial needs. In the next subsection, the accounting organization structure is reviewed. Such questions as: "Is the organization structure compatible with accounting by profit centers?" and "Is the accounting structure flexible enough to accommodate business changes?" are typical ones to be answered.

Within the leadership subsection, the focus is on the capability of accounting management to exert the necessary direction to meet accounting objectives and deadlines. Also, reference is made to supplying needed information to control the operating environment. Supplementary to this subsection is one on communication, whose focus is on the communication of accounting information to management and operating personnel. The last subsection (accounting control questions) examines how meaningful the various accounting management reports are to their recipients. Overall, the accounting section of the management audit questionnaire aids in evaluating how well this functional area meets the managerial demands placed upon it.

Finance

Evaluation of an organization's finance function through a management audit questionnaire builds upon the accounting section set forth previously. Questions relating to long-range finance plans center on the capability of the organization to finance its future operations under changing conditions. Consideration is given to comparing the company to other companies in the same field. The same kinds of questions are applied to short- or medium-range finance plans. As with the long-range finance plans, these questions ultimately evaluate the quality of finance management to meet predetermined objectives. To accomplish stated financial plans, the organization structure should be flexible enough to meet changing business conditions. Also, finance procedures should be an integral part of the information system that assists management in meeting its objectives.

Related to the foregoing subsections of the questionnaire are questions treating the leadership qualities of finance management. Emphasis is placed upon financial management's ability to maximize the company's return on its investment in various assets and minimizing the liabilities owed. Akin to the leadership subsection is the evaluation of the effectiveness of communication of financial information. Emphasis is placed on communicating appropriate financial information to the various management levels. The last subsection assesses the adequacy of financial/managerial reports, methods, and procedures for controlling present and future operations. Also, this final section examines the treasurer's capability to exert sufficient control over financial matters to meet predetermined organization objectives.

Application of Management Audit Questionnaire to Cost Control

Yesterday, the controller of the XYZ Company was confronted in the hallway with some rather harsh words from the vice president of marketing about the accuracy of the company's cost figures for setting selling prices. Unfortunately, the executive did not have time to elaborate on the matter because he was leaving on a two-week vacation. Since the company wants to be competitive, it makes every attempt to keep selling prices as low as possible. Actual company costs and proposed wage increases, plus factors for profit and inflation, are utilized for setting selling prices. In this manner, marketing management feels it has a real handle on what is a fair price for its products.

Because of the charge that cost figures (standard costs) are unreliable, the controller immediately called a meeting with the company's head cost accountant about this problem. During the course of the meeting, both men went over the procedures for costing products and found them to be in line with company policy—that is, in-process standards on manufactured items are totaled to include raw materials and labor before applying factory overhead. However, the controller felt that the *real* problem was not uncovered during the meeting, so he handed the problem over to the company's outside auditors, who were in the process of completing interim work. Although the controller could have taken the time to uncover the problem, he felt that, in view of the seriousness of the charge, an objective viewpoint by outsiders would be well worth its cost.

As a starting point, the outside auditors decided to use the accounting section of the management audit questionnaire. The completed section, shown in Figure 4-2, contains several negative answers that need to be analyzed further.

Although the first few questions on flexible budgets are answered with yes, the sixth and seventh questions relating to management control center reports and cost reports are answered in the negative because these reports do not provide meaningful operating information to managers, particularly, company foremen. A visit to the closest manufacturing plant by the outside

Figure 4-2. XYZ Company evaluation of control of product costs, using the accounting and finance management audit questionnaire.

	YES	NO	N.A.
ACCOUNTING			
F. Control:			
1. Are accounting/management control reports:			
a. timely?	X		
b. simple to use?	X		
c. properly designed?	X		
2. Are budgets stated on a flexible (variable) basis to reflect current conditions?	X		
3. Are flexible budgets used effectively by managers?	X		
4. Is the management by exception principle employed for flexible budgets?	X		
5. Are flexible budgets of the following types prepared:			
a. cash?	X		
b. operating?	X		
c. capital?	X		
d. work center?	X		
e. others, as deemed necessary?	X		
6. Do management control center reports provide meaningful operating information to managers?		X	
7. Do cost accounting reports provide meaningful cost analysis information to managers?		X	
8. Is intelligent use made of cost data in:			
a. setting sales prices?		X	
b. valuing inventories?		X	
c. preparing financial statements?		X	
d. controlling operations?		X	
e. determining cost-volume relationships?		X	
9. If products are unprofitable, is this information communicated to the proper authorities?	X		
10. Is control exercised by management over *controllable* costs, such as direct materials and direct labor?		X	
11. Is control exercised by management over *period* costs, such as insurance and personal property taxes?	X		
12. Is there sufficient managerial control over:			
a. accounts receivable?	X		
b. bad debts?	X		

c. fixed assets?	X	__	__
d. other assets?	X	__	__
e. accounts payable?	X	__	__
f. other payables?	X	__	__
13. Are there effective internal accounting control (details equal summary) procedures in use?	__	X	__
14. Are there effective internal check (one or more persons checking on each other) procedures in use?	X	__	__

Questionnaire Comments (Negative Answers):

Question 6 Because of recent abnormal increases of basic raw materials, management control center reports at the plant level do not provide meaningful operating information to company foremen.

Question 7 Cost accounting reports normally provide meaningful cost analysis information to managers, but these recent abnormal price increases have not been included in cost standards.

Question 8 Because of these price increases, cost data have been misused in the setting of sales prices, among others.

Question 10 Since variances between actual and standard costs are ignored for the most part at the foreman and supervisory levels, very little, if any, attempt is exercised to oversee controllable costs.

Question 13 Internal accounting control procedures have failed to bring to light the unfortunate condition of ignoring reported operational cost variances of in-process items.

---

auditors disclosed this critical factor. Because of the recent increases of several basic raw material prices that were not reflected in the appropriate cost standards, unfavorable variances between actual and standard costs of in-process items had become common at the plant level. In addition, the control system failed to pinpoint these variances caused by high raw-materials prices, as well as other variances caused by production. After a short period, plant foremen and supervisors, knowing that many of the cost standards for in-process items were unrealistic and unattainable, ignored the variance information.

In addition, the negative answer to question 8 indicates that cost data do not provide meaningful information for setting sales prices, valuing inventories, preparing financial statements, controlling operations, and determining cost–volume relationships. Similarly, question 10 is indicative of the negative attitude of plant personnel toward supervising controllable costs closely. The negative answer to question 13 shows that effective accounting control procedures are not operating to bring this unfavorable condition to light at the plant level.

The remaining questions in Figure 4-2 were answered in the affirmative. Even though not shown in this case study, appropriate sections of the management audit questionnaire were completed to ensure that all facets of the cost problem had been examined before making final recommendations to the controller.

Recommendations to Improve Cost Control

The cost control difficulties in the plant were not hard for the experienced outside auditors to detect. However, developing appropriate recommendations in the form of cost control procedures took a little more time. After several meetings with plant supervisors, foremen, and accounting and computer personnel, the auditors suggested that more frequent updating procedures be initiated, that is, cost data stored on computerized files should be updated weekly instead of quarterly. In this manner, when standard costs are compared to actual costs for in-process manufactured items, their total costs of material and labor will serve as a valid basis for comparison.

Although this recommendation solves the immediate problem, the engineering department also needs to investigate the possibility of using lower-priced raw materials. The outside auditors further recommended that, if this is not possible, the manufactured parts be redesigned to take advantage of lower-priced materials. Such an approach will enable the company to remain competitive and, in some cases, beat the prices of its competitors.

Additionally, a recommendation was made regarding the possibility of storing the cost data for in-process items on-line within the computerized information system so that cost data would always be up to date. With the implementation of such an approach, the problem of out-of-date standard cost figures should never recur.

Application of Management Audit Questionnaire to Financial Control

Recently, the vice president in charge of accounting and finance for the XYZ Company received an internal control letter from the CPA firm that audits the company's financial statements. The outside auditors were critical of one aspect of internal accounting control, namely, the fact that certain subsidiary ledgers did not agree with the totals maintained in the general ledger.

On the basis of this objective observation, the vice president directed the company's assistant treasurer to investigate this claim by utilizing the accounting and finance management audit questionnaire (see Figure 4-3). This task took the assistant treasurer three weeks, since this project was undertaken in addition to his normal duties. A thorough analysis of the facts disclosed that, on occasion, the subsidiary ledgers did indeed not agree with the control totals. In every case where this occurred, it was determined that the individuals responsible for the detail had been on vacation. Upon their return, appropriate corrections were invariably made to bring the detail into agreement with the control total. Hence, in all situation, lack of trained personnel led to these differences for a very short time period. In essence, the foregoing problem was not really a big one, since all corrections were made before period closings.

Although the foregoing problem was relatively easy to diagnose and explain to the vice president, the assistant treasurer uncovered a much larger problem when answering the questions for the control subsection of the finance section. As noted in Figure 4-3, question 7 has been answered with no. The accounts payable clerks, knowing that vendor invoices are paid every 15 days (15th and 30th), take discounts offered on payment with 15 days and over. In contrast, those discounts offered on payment under 15 days are rejected, since the company would not be able to pay the bills in time. Thus invoices received with terms such as 2/10, n/30 (2 percent discount if paid within 10 days, no discount allowable if paid up to 30 days), never earned a discount for the company.

Recommendations to Improve Financial Control

In this case study, the management audit questionnaire has been used to uncover an important problem that was not included initially in the investigation. This can be expected to happen when a management audit is undertaken, because the questionnaire is very comprehensive.

The assistant treasurer's recommendations took several directions. First, he recommended that all major vendors with which the company was experiencing this problem of under 15 days for the discount period be contacted. All vendors except two agreed to allow the discount if the bill was paid at the next payment date—the 15th or 30th of the month for the XYZ Company. Second, all personnel who work full- or part-time in preparing vendor invoices for payment are to undergo on-the-job training so that all legitimate discounts are taken. Third, the internal auditor is to check periodically so as to ensure that the discount earned is proper. Lastly, the assistant treasurer recommended that the accounting and finance part of the management audit questionnaire be utilized by the outside auditors as a part of their annual audit. All of these recommendations were approved by the vice president in charge of accounting and finance.

Figure 4-3. XYZ Company evaluation of control of finance, using the accounting and finance management audit questionnaire.

	YES	NO	N.A.
FINANCE			
F. Control:			
1. Does the treasurer exert sufficient control so that the company maintains a sound financial position?	X		
2. Does the treasurer exert sufficient control over cash flow to:			
a. maximize its usage?	X		
b. pay the company's obligations?	X		
3. Does the treasurer exert sufficient influence so that company taxes are kept as low as possible?	X		
4. Are financial/managerial reports, methods, and techniques used, including:			
a. cash forecasts?	X		
b. balance sheet?	X		
c. income statement?	X		
d. management control center reports?	X		
e. source and application of funds statement?	X		
f. budgets?	X		
g. financial ratios?	X		
h. break-even analysis?	X		
i. return on investment?	X		
j. costing methods?	X		
5. Are financial control reports prepared on a basis that provides for changing conditions?	X		
6. Is there an adequate cash balance to take advantage of discounts offered on purchased items?	X		
7. Is adequate control maintained over discounts offered on purchased items?		X	
8. Are discounted cash flow or similar methods used to evaluate capital expenditures?	X		
9. Is the management by exception principle utilized for financial/managerial control reports, methods, and techniques?	X		

Questionnaire Comment (Negative Answer):
Question 7   Although discounts of 15 days and over are taken on purchased items, the same cannot be said for discounts under 15 days.

SUMMARY

In this chapter, the accounting and finance part of the management audit questionnaire was presented. It was divided into the following sections: I. Accounting and Finance Overview, II. Accounting, and III. Finance. As in the prior chapter, selected subsections of the questionnaire were applied to the XYZ Company. These subsections provide a means for an objective third party to analyze the facts and define the real problem. In turn, constructive recommendations can be made to overcome the deficiencies identified so that organization objectives can be more fully realized.

III

MANAGEMENT AUDITING

of
Marketing- and
Service-Oriented
Functional Areas

5

Evaluating the Marketing Function

THE MARKETING FUNCTION tends to be more difficult to evaluate by utilizing a management audit questionnaire than most other functional areas. The principal reason is that marketing is highly dependent upon external environmental factors that are not under the control of marketing management. Typical examples include the prices of competitors, the general level of economic activity, and the rate of inflation. Similarly, marketing is often dependent upon human judgment, involved with complex relationships, and beset with imperfect knowledge, resulting in decisions being made by sheer intuition rather than by some type of scientific analysis. Although experience and intuition are vital ingredients in marketing, they can be greatly enhanced by computer analysis and quantitative techniques. No matter what viewpoint, or what combination of the two approaches—intuitional and quantitative—is found within an organization, the five sections of the marketing management audit questionnaire (see Figure 5-1), namely:

    I. Marketing Overview
    II. Sales
    III. Market Research
    IV. Advertising
    V. Physical Distribution

are broad enough to make the questionnaire adaptable to most situations.

Following the presentation and discussion of the marketing questionnaire, two sample applications will be demonstrated for the XYZ Company, the text's master case study. These applications center on long-range marketing plans and market research leadership.

(text continues on page 103)

Figure 5-1. Management Audit Questionnaire: Marketing.

	YES	NO	N.A.

I. MARKETING OVERVIEW

  A. Long-Range Plans:

    1. Are long-range marketing plans in agreement with:

      a. long-range organization objectives?   ___ ___ ___

      b. long-range plans of other functional areas?   ___ ___ ___

      c. medium-range marketing plans?   ___ ___ ___

      d. short-range marketing plans?   ___ ___ ___

    2. Are long-range marketing plans reviewed by:

      a. board of directors?   ___ ___ ___

      b. top management?   ___ ___ ___

    3. Do long-range marketing plans include the following functional areas:

      a. sales?   ___ ___ ___

      b. market research?   ___ ___ ___

      c. advertising?   ___ ___ ___

      d. physical distribution?   ___ ___ ___

    4. Is there an official planning committee to develop long-range marketing plans?   ___ ___ ___

    5. Does marketing management accept and understand these long-range plans?   ___ ___ ___

    6. Are marketing management efforts directed toward accomplishing these long-range plans?   ___ ___ ___

    7. Is performance against long-range marketing plans measured periodically?   ___ ___ ___

    8. Are long-range marketing plans reviewed periodically so as to stay current?   ___ ___ ___

    9. Have forecasts been sufficiently accurate to develop long-range marketing plans?   ___ ___ ___

    10. Is the management by exception principle an integral part of long-range marketing plans?   ___ ___ ___

  B. Short- or Medium-Range Plans:

    1. Are short- or medium-range marketing plans in agreement with:

	YES	NO	N.A.
a. short- or medium-range organization objectives?	____	____	____
b. short- or medium-range plans of other functional areas?	____	____	____
c. long-range marketing plans?	____	____	____
2. Are short- or medium-range marketing plans reviewed by:			
a. top management?	____	____	____
b. middle management?	____	____	____
c. lower management?	____	____	____
3. Do short- or medium-range marketing plans include the following functional areas:			
a. sales?	____	____	____
b. market research?	____	____	____
c. advertising?	____	____	____
d. physical distribution?	____	____	____
4. Are there procedures for developing short- or medium-range marketing plans?	____	____	____
5. Does marketing management accept and understand these short- or medium-range plans?	____	____	____
6. Are marketing management efforts directed toward accomplishing these short- or medium-range plans?	____	____	____
7. Is performance against short- or medium-range plans measured periodically?	____	____	____
8. Are short- or medium-range marketing plans reviewed periodically to stay current?	____	____	____
9. Have forecasts been sufficiently accurate to develop short- or medium-range marketing plans?	____	____	____
10. Is the management by exception principle an integral part of short- or medium-range marketing plans?	____	____	____

C. Organization Structure:

1. Is the marketing organization structure adequate to fulfill stated marketing:			
a. objectives?	____	____	____
b. plans?	____	____	____
c. strategies?	____	____	____
d. programs?	____	____	____
e. policies?	____	____	____
2. Is the marketing organization chart compatible with other functional organization charts?	____	____	____

	YES	NO	N.A.
3. Is it clear who is charged with responsibility and who has authority over:			
a. sales?	—	—	—
b. market research?	—	—	—
c. advertising?	—	—	—
d. physical distribution?	—	—	—
4. Does each marketing person know his or her job well?	—	—	—
5. Is it clear what the superior–subordinate relationships are in the marketing department?	—	—	—
6. Are there adequate job descriptions for each marketing position?	—	—	—
7. Is there a competent employee assigned to each marketing position?	—	—	—
8. Can the quality of marketing personnel be assessed for:			
a. management?	—	—	—
b. employees?	—	—	—
9. Is the marketing department adequately staffed?	—	—	—
10. Are reporting relationships clearly defined and understood by marketing personnel?	—	—	—
11. Is marketing management held accountable for its actions?	—	—	—
12. Is there provision within the marketing department for periodic review of its organization structure?	—	—	—

D. Leadership:

	YES	NO	N.A.
1. Does marketing management provide the leadership to develop:			
a. new product opportunities?	—	—	—
b. new market segments?	—	—	—
c. new promotional ideas?	—	—	—
2. Is some form of leadership evident in these marketing areas:			
a. sales?	—	—	—
b. market research?	—	—	—
c. advertising?	—	—	—
d. physical distribution?	—	—	—
3. Is marketing management sufficiently progressive to take a chance on a new product?	—	—	—
4. Is the organization's marketing program geared to leadership in the marketplace?	—	—	—

YES   NO   N.A.

5. Does marketing management provide the know-how to meet competition head on?   ___   ___   ___

E. Communication:

1. Have short- to long-range marketing objectives and plans been communicated to the proper marketing personnel?   ___   ___   ___
2. Have the organization's marketing strategies and programs been communicated to the proper marketing personnel?   ___   ___   ___
3. Have the organization's marketing policies been communicated to the proper marketing personnel?   ___   ___   ___
4. Are communication channels adequate for the coordination of marketing activities, namely, in regard to:
   a. new product introductions?   ___   ___   ___
   b. pricing policies?   ___   ___   ___
   c. personal selling practices?   ___   ___   ___
   d. special promotions?   ___   ___   ___
   e. market research studies?   ___   ___   ___
   f. advertising programs?   ___   ___   ___
   g. physical distribution methods?   ___   ___   ___
5. Is there effective feedback of important marketing information to the proper personnel?   ___   ___   ___

F. Control:

1. Do the managers of marketing activities exercise sufficient control to achieve desired marketing objectives in these areas:
   a. sales?   ___   ___   ___
   b. market research?   ___   ___   ___
   c. advertising?   ___   ___   ___
   d. physical distribution?   ___   ___   ___
2. Are effective control reports, methods, and techniques utilized for these marketing areas:
   a. sales?   ___   ___   ___
   b. market research?   ___   ___   ___
   c. advertising?   ___   ___   ___
   d. physical distribution?   ___   ___   ___
3. Is close control maintained over marketing activities and their costs?   ___   ___   ___

YES   NO   N.A.

4. Are marketing goals compared to actual results (budget versus actual):
   a. on a periodic basis?   ____ ____ ____
   b. on a timely basis?   ____ ____ ____
5. Is corrective action undertaken when significant marketing deviations are detected?   ____ ____ ____

II. SALES   ____ ____ ____

A. Long-Range Plans:

1. Is sales management of sufficient caliber to meet long-range sales objectives?   ____ ____ ____
2. Have sales been adequate over the long run to meet organization objectives?   ____ ____ ____
3. Has the organization maintained its *past* share of the total market?   ____ ____ ____
4. Does the organization have a strategy for maintaining its *future* share of the total market?   ____ ____ ____
5. Do long-range plans include the leveling out of sales peaks and valleys?   ____ ____ ____
6. Are sales forecasting techniques:
   a. used?   ____ ____ ____
   b. adequate?   ____ ____ ____
7. Does the organization calculate long-range data for products by:
   a. sales volumes?   ____ ____ ____
   b. contribution factors?   ____ ____ ____
   c. breakeven points?   ____ ____ ____
8. Are long-range sales quotas established for:
   a. products or product lines?   ____ ____ ____
   b. sales or geographical areas?   ____ ____ ____
   c. salespersons?   ____ ____ ____
9. Are the organization's products or product lines diversified?   ____ ____ ____
10. Does the organization have a policy on developing new products?   ____ ____ ____
11. Is this policy adequate for developing future growth?   ____ ____ ____
12. Is there an adequate long-range program for developing the sales force in the future?   ____ ____ ____
13. Are sales service policies adequate for future growth?   ____ ____ ____
14. Are the organization's products relevant to the times?   ____ ____ ____

	YES	NO	N.A.

15. Does the organization have advantages over its competition in the long run? ____ ____ ____
16. Are there adequate incentive programs to keep sales at a desired level? ____ ____ ____
17. Does the sales compensation plan encourage long-range sales as well as immediate sales? ____ ____ ____

B. Short- or Medium-Range Plans:
   1. Do the organization's short- or medium-range plans highlight its advantages over its competition in:
      a. product innovation? ____ ____ ____
      b. merchandising capabilities? ____ ____ ____
      c. advertising effectiveness? ____ ____ ____
      d. personal selling expertise? ____ ____ ____
      e. other marketing factors deemed necessary? ____ ____ ____
   2. Are there well-defined policies included within the organization's marketing short- or medium-range plans on:
      a. sales? ____ ____ ____
      b. returns? ____ ____ ____
      c. allowances? ____ ____ ____
      d. commissions? ____ ____ ____
   3. Are short- or medium-range sales forecasting techniques:
      a. used? ____ ____ ____
      b. adequate? ____ ____ ____
   4. Are there short- or medium-range sales quotas? ____ ____ ____
   5. Are sales performance records maintained by:
      a. products or product lines? ____ ____ ____
      b. sales or geographical areas? ____ ____ ____
      c. salespersons? ____ ____ ____
      d. advertising effectiveness? ____ ____ ____
   6. Are selling efforts directed toward those products with high unit contribution? ____ ____ ____
   7. Are short- or medium-range plans directed toward a sales mix that maximizes:
      a. satisfaction of customer needs? ____ ____ ____
      b. customer service? ____ ____ ____
      c. profits? ____ ____ ____

	YES	NO	N.A.

8. Is the short- or medium-range sales program directed toward, at least, maintaining the company's share of the market?

9. Do the short- or medium-range sales plans include a program to maintain or improve its customer relations?

10. Are selling prices established on a sound financial basis?

11. Does the pricing mechanism provide a satisfactory return for the:
    a. manufacturer?
    b. distributor?
    c. retailer?

12. Does the pricing mechanism provide for:
    a. inflationary or deflationary times?
    b. volume variations?
    c. unforeseen contingencies?

13. Is there adequate sales supervision to accomplish short- or medium-range sales goals?

14. Are there adequate salespersons to meet short- or medium-range sales goals?

15. Do short- or medium-range sales plans include an effective sales training program?

C. Organization Structure:

1. Are sales quotas established for each:
   a. sales area?
   b. product or product line?
   c. salesperson?

2. Are sales and service policies structured for short- to long-term growth?

3. Are sales and service policies sufficiently flexible to meet short- to long-term growth?

4. Are sales and service policies sufficiently flexible to meet changing business conditions?

5. Are there individual product-line sales managers?

6. Is there adequate sales personnel in the field?

	YES	NO	N.A.

7. Is the organization's sales compensation plan structured so that it encourages:
   a. immediate sales? ___ ___ ___
   b. intermediate sales? ___ ___ ___
   c. long-term sales? ___ ___ ___
8. Is the organization's sales compensation plan structured so that it is effective as to the:
   a. amount? ___ ___ ___
   b. incentive? ___ ___ ___
   c. method? ___ ___ ___

D. Leadership:
   1. Does sales management spend ample time in the field to provide advice and support to sales personnel? ___ ___ ___
   2. Does sales management instill in its salespersons a sense of being sales-oriented? ___ ___ ___
   3. Are salespersons sufficiently motivated by sales management to reach their sales quotas? ___ ___ ___
   4. Does sales management solicit ideas and opinions about new products from its salespersons and make constructive use of them? ___ ___ ___
   5. Do salespersons feel completely free to discuss their problems with sales management? ___ ___ ___
   6. Is there a friendly interaction, with a high degree of confidence and trust, between sales management and salespersons? ___ ___ ___
   7. Are salespersons involved in important decisions that affect their sales efforts? ___ ___ ___
   8. Are salespersons adequately trained to meet the challenge presented to them? ___ ___ ___

E. Communication:
   1. Are *downward* and *upward* communication channels used effectively to keep salespersons abreast of overall organizational activities that may have some effect on their sales efforts? ___ ___ ___
   2. Have sales quotas been communicated to all salespersons? ___ ___ ___
   3. Are weekly sales reports communicated from the field to sales management? ___ ___ ___

YES   NO   N.A.

4. Are sales and service policies communicated to salespersons? ___ ___ ___

5. Are salespersons' bulletins, issued on a periodic basis, an effective means of communication, i.e., are they read and is appropriate action taken when required? ___ ___ ___

6. Are new methods and techniques of selling communicated to salespersons? ___ ___ ___

7. Are salespersons kept abreast of finished-goods inventories that need to be sold before they spoil, deteriorate, or lose their value? ___ ___ ___

8. Are salespersons kept abreast of excess finished-goods inventories that need to be sold? ___ ___ ___

F. Control:

1. Does sales management exercise effective control over:
   a. personal selling? ___ ___ ___
   b. advertising? ___ ___ ___
   c. regular promotions? ___ ___ ___
   d. special promotions? ___ ___ ___

2. Is close control exercised by sales management over these areas:
   a. sales goals? ___ ___ ___
   b. sales prices? ___ ___ ___
   c. sales returns? ___ ___ ___
   d. sales allowances? ___ ___ ___

3. Is sales performance controlled by:
   a. products or product lines? ___ ___ ___
   b. sales or geographical areas? ___ ___ ___
   c. salespersons? ___ ___ ___

4. Are sales control reports, methods, and techniques:
   a. used? ___ ___ ___
   b. adequate? ___ ___ ___

5. Where there are deviations between sales goals and actual sales, does sales management undertake corrective action when deemed necessary? ___ ___ ___

6. Is there adequate sales supervision in the field to control ongoing sales activities? ___ ___ ___

7. Are adequate field sales reports forwarded to sales management for better control of the organization's sales efforts? ___ ___ ___

	YES	NO	N.A.

8. Is there effective control by sales management over product selling prices?

9. Does sales management exercise sufficient control to at least maintain the organization's share of the market?

10. Does sales management exercise adequate control to maintain or improve customer relations?

11. Is there sufficient control exercised over the sales compensation program to ensure equitable:
   a. sales commissions?
   b. sales bonuses?

12. Do controls exist for monitoring the quantity and dollar value of customer orders that are behind schedule?

III. MARKET RESEARCH

A. Long-Range Plans:

1. Are long-range market research plans compatible with overall marketing plans?

2. Is there a clear-cut division of responsibility between sales and market research?

3. Is market research management capable of handling long-term research projects?

4. Are long-term market research projects adequately funded?

5. Is the market research department for long-term projects adequately:
   a. supervised?
   b. staffed?

6. Are markets studied in depth before new product development?

7. Are the organization's present products or product lines studied to indicate their relationship to continual shifting:
   a. geographical trends?
   b. market potential?
   c. disposable income?

8. Are long-range statistics available for the following characteristics of the population that form the potential market for the organization's products:

	YES	NO	N.A.
a. buying habits?	___	___	___
b. number in family?	___	___	___
c. type of housing?	___	___	___
d. type of transportation?	___	___	___

B. Short- or Medium-Range Plans:

1. Are short- or medium-term market research projects an integral part of the current year's budget?   ___ ___ ___
2. Are short- or medium-term market research projects for reliable results adequately:
   a. supervised?   ___ ___ ___
   b. staffed?   ___ ___ ___
3. Is the market research group sufficiently flexible to make changes in its ongoing projects?   ___ ___ ___
4. Is the market research group consulted in the planning of:
   a. sales quotas?   ___ ___ ___
   b. product distributions?   ___ ___ ___
   c. retail promotions?   ___ ___ ___
5. Does ongoing market research utilize current data in evaluating new products?   ___ ___ ___
6. Are new market research methods and techniques employed by market research management and its staff?   ___ ___ ___

C. Organization Structure:

1. Are market structures studied before new product development?   ___ ___ ___
2. Are the changing structural characteristics of markets studied, such as trends back to cities and shifts of markets from one income level to another?   ___ ___ ___
3. Are statistics generated regarding the characteristics of population comprising potential customers for the organization's products, such as income, number in the family, and buying habits?   ___ ___ ___
4. Are market areas analyzed on the basis of sales potential and desired market share?   ___ ___ ___
5. Are market structures checked periodically for weak and strong areas?   ___ ___ ___

YES   NO   N.A.

D. Leadership:

1. Is the market research group under the direction of capable and progressive management?

2. Does market research management make its presence felt in planning:
   a. sales quotas?
   b. advertising?
   c. physical distribution?

3. Does market research management require that the dynamics of the marketplace, i.e., trends to the suburbs, shifts of market potential, be incorporated in market research studies?

4. Is market research management capable of exerting influence to get desired market statistics regarding characteristics of the population, i.e., income, number in the family, and buying habits?

5. Is market research management capable of exerting sufficient influence to analyze market areas on the basis of sales potential and desired market shares?

6. Does market research management exert sufficient influence to make new statistical tools available to its staff?

E. Communication:

1. Does market research management communicate new ideas on marketing projects to its staff?

2. Are long-range marketing plans communicated to the market research group so that they may be incorporated as a part of specific market research projects?

3. Are the latest product sales data communicated to the market research group through the organization's information system?

4. Within the market research group, is there a free exchange of ideas:
   a. among peers?
   b. with their superiors?

YES   NO   N.A.

5. Do organization personnel communicate information on ideas for possible new product development to the market research group? ___ ___ ___

6. Do sales personnel communicate important changes in the marketplace to market research personnel? ___ ___ ___

7. Are important market research data compiled by government and/or private agencies communicated to market researchers? ___ ___ ___

F. Control:

1. Are market research studies adequately controlled by market research management? ___ ___ ___

2. Are adequate controls established over market research projects? ___ ___ ___

3. Is there an effort to keep market research costs under control? ___ ___ ___

4. Are deviations from budgeted market research costs analyzed by market research management? ___ ___ ___

5. Are weak sales areas researched adequately so as to uncover their deficiencies? ___ ___ ___

6. Are weak products researched adequately so as to uncover their deficiencies? ___ ___ ___

IV. ADVERTISING ___ ___ ___

A. Long-Range Plans:

1. Is the advertising program an integral part of long-range marketing plans? ___ ___ ___

2. Is the advertising .budget adequately managed to meet long-range plans? ___ ___ ___

3. Are regular promotions, salespersons' contests, etc. an integral part of the long-range advertising program? ___ ___ ___

4. Are seasonal promotions integrated with long-range plans? ___ ___ ___

B. Short- or Medium-Range Plans:

1. Is the advertising budget adequately managed to meet short- or medium-range plans? ___ ___ ___

2. Is there a well-planned advertising program for the short or medium run? ___ ___ ___

	YES	NO	N.A.

3. Are regular promotions, salespersons' contests, etc. an integral part of the short- or medium-range advertising program?   — — —

4. Are there seasonal promotions to overcome sales fluctuations?   — — —

C. Organization Structure:

1. Is the advertising budget adequate to meet current sales objectives?   — — —

2. Are advertising budgets established for:
   a. each product or product line?   — — —
   b. each sales area?   — — —

3. Are advertising policies structured for short- to long-term growth?   — — —

4. Can the advertising budget be adjusted to reflect constantly changing economic conditions?   — — —

5. Is there provision for correction by advertising management when advertising costs exceed the budget?   — — —

6. Is advertising integrated with personal selling and promotion?   — — —

D. Leadership:

1. Is the organization recognized as a leader in innovative advertising?   — — —

2. Is advertising management capable of developing a well-thought-out and well-integrated advertising program?   — — —

3. Is advertising management capable of developing regular promotions and salespersons' contests that are an integral part of the organization's total advertising program?   — — —

4. Does advertising management develop seasonal promotions to overcome seasonal sales fluctuations?   — — —

5. Is advertising management progressive enough to relate its advertising message to the current times?   — — —

E. Communication:

1. Is advertising management communicating advertising messages that are relevant to the times?   — — —

2. Are the advantages of the organization's products over its competition adequately communicated to its customers?   — — —

YES   NO   N.A.

3. Is the organization's advertising program effective in communicating its intended messages on:
a. regular promotions? ____ ____ ____
b. special promotions? ____ ____ ____
4. Are advertising and special promotion
expenses in line with personal selling
expenses so that there is a balance in
the overall marketing program? ____ ____ ____
5. Are salespersons' contests integrated
with overall advertising efforts so that
maximum effectiveness is derived from
these marketing efforts? ____ ____ ____
6. Are quantitative and statistical techniques employed to determine the best
means of reaching specific market segments for certain products? ____ ____ ____

F. Control:
1. Is there an effort made by advertising
management to eliminate ineffective advertising? ____ ____ ____
2. Is there an effort made by advertising
management to keep advertising costs
within the budget? ____ ____ ____
3. Is corrective action undertaken by advertising management when advertising
costs exceed budget amounts? ____ ____ ____
4. Is advertising sufficiently controlled so
that erratic sales fluctuations are kept
to a minimum? ____ ____ ____
5. Are the latest quantitative and statistical
techniques employed to make sure that
the organization gets the most out of its
advertising expenditures? ____ ____ ____

V. PHYSICAL DISTRIBUTION ____ ____ ____

A. Long-Range Plans:
1. Is physical distribution an integral part
of long-range marketing plans? ____ ____ ____
2. Is physical distribution management active in the preparation of its long-range
plans? ____ ____ ____
3. Are distributors large enough to handle
anticipated future volume? ____ ____ ____
4. Is there a periodic evaluation of distributors to assess their contribution to the
physical distribution system? ____ ____ ____

	YES	NO	N.A.

5. Have distribution costs been in line with the industry?

6. Will there be thorough retail coverage in the future, particularly, in key market areas?

7. Are there continuing educational programs to aid distributors in moving larger volumes in the future?

B. Short- or Medium-Range Plans:

1. Is physical distribution management aware and capable of solving its short- or medium-range problems?

2. Do short- or medium-range plans include provision for meeting scheduled delivery dates?

3. Are distribution centers staffed by properly trained personnel?

4. Are distribution centers strategically located near large population centers?

5. Do current policies and programs aid the distributors in managing their operations effectively with respect to:
   a. sales promotion?
   b. advertising?
   c. dealer aids?

6. Do short- or medium-range plans include continuing programs to assist distributors and retailers in moving products?

C. Organization Structure:

1. Is there an adequate number of distribution centers to handle:
   a. present volume?
   b. anticipated future volume?

2. Are key marketing areas structured so that they are adequately serviced by efficient distribution centers?

3. Is the distribution system organized so that there is a thorough retail coverage, particularly in key areas?

4. Is the organization structured so that there are continuing programs to aid distribution centers and retailers in having a high turnover of inventory?

YES   NO   N.A.

5. Is the organization structured so that there are policies and programs designed to aid distribution centers and retailers with respect to:
   a. sales promotion?   ___ ___ ___
   b. advertising?   ___ ___ ___
   c. profitability?   ___ ___ ___
6. Are physical distribution programs sufficiently flexible to accommodate changing conditions?   ___ ___ ___

D. Leadership:

1. Does physical distribution management assist its distribution channels in achieving a high merchandise turnover?   ___ ___ ___
2. Are distribution channels utilized that keep physical distribution costs at a minimum?   ___ ___ ___
3. Is the organization sufficiently flexible to change distribution channels when they no longer serve its needs?   ___ ___ ___
4. Does distribution management recognize current and imminent changes affecting distribution channels?   ___ ___ ___
5. Does the organization have programs to aid its distribution channels in their management?   ___ ___ ___
6. Does distribution management require that company-owned goods be handled and stored properly for fast shipment to customers?   ___ ___ ___

E. Communication:

1. Does distribution management communicate coming distribution changes to the organization's planning group?   ___ ___ ___
2. Are inadequacies of the present physical distribution system communicated to top management for correction?   ___ ___ ___
3. Are organization policies and programs to aid distributors communicated to them in an effective manner?   ___ ___ ___
4. Do distribution channels feed back essential information for maintaining an effective physical distribution system?   ___ ___ ___
5. Are there effective procedures to alert distribution management that certain products are not being moved as fast as planned?   ___ ___ ___

	YES	NO	N.A.

F. Control:

1. Is there an effort by physical distribution management to keep distribution costs under control? ___ ___ ___
2. Is there adequate control over programs to aid retailers in promoting the organization's products? ___ ___ ___
3. Is there adequate control over finished-goods inventory:
   a. on hand? ___ ___ ___
   b. in the hands of distributors? ___ ___ ___
4. Does control over finished goods include a program to aid retailers in increasing inventory turnover? ___ ___ ___
5. Is corrective action undertaken by physical distribution management when exceptions are uncovered? ___ ___ ___

COMMENTS ON THE MARKETING QUESTIONNAIRE

Marketing Overview

No matter what type of business organization, marketing generally starts the information flow from customers desiring specifc goods and/or services. Not only does marketing receive orders from customers, but also marketing efforts are focused on them. The company's marketing executives derive their information about customers and the marketplace through marketing intelligence, formal market research, and company accounting information. Marketing intelligence activity represents the continuous effort to keep informed about current developments among customers, competing products, and the marketing environment. In a similar manner, market research centers on a more formal approach to current developments, in particular, project-oriented research. The company's accounting system generates sales and cost information to complement marketing intelligence and research. Overall, marketing management needs an effective information flow to relate its efforts to constantly changing conditions.

The purpose of this initial section of the marketing management audit questionnaire it two-fold. First, this section concentrates on the ability of marketing management to meet changing environmental factors, both external and internal. The manner in which marketing management relates to changing environmental factors is one way of determining how well it is prepared to meet the challenges of changing times. The proper meshing of the external and internal environments with an organization's business functions, particularly marketing, leads to efficiency and economy of organizational operations for accomplishing predetermined objectives. Second, this section determines the degree of integration of the marketing function with other functional areas that relate to marketing.

Sales

Evaluation of an organization's sales effort through the management audit questionnaire (see Figure 5-1, section II) starts with examining the capabilities of sales management. Questions on long-range marketing plans with respect to such items as products, services, policies, and salesperson compensation are set forth. Similar questions are asked about short- or medium-range marketing plans. As with long-range sales plans, these questions ultimately evaluate the ability of an organization's sales management to perform its assigned tasks. Specifically, emphasis is placed on the ability of sales managers to meet sales quotas that not only result in profitable operations, but also increase customer satisfaction and keep salespersons sufficiently motivated to meet new sales goals. Enlarging upon this last point, the sales organization structure should be flexible enough to meet both short- and long-term sales growth objectives and changing business conditions. Likewise, the sales compensation plan should encourage both immediate and longer-term sales.

Building upon the above subsections of the questionnaire, questions relating to sales management leadership are developed. Emphasis is placed on the effectiveness of sales management in getting the sales staff to achieve specific sales goals. Also, the degree of confidence and trust between sales managers and salespersons is assessed. Complementary to leadership is an evaluation of sales management's communication skills, with particular emphasis on critical information needed to keep salespersons abreast of important organizational activities. In the final subsection, the degree of sales control exercised by sales management is reviewed—that is, how well sales goals are related to actual sales so that corrective action can be undertaken if results are below expectations.

Market Research

Before extensive new product development is undertaken, it is helpful to initiate a market research study to determine the feasibility of bringing a new product to the marketplace. The first subsection of the market research section (see section III of Figure 5-1) evaluates the effects of long-range plans on market research. In like manner, the relationships of short- or medium-range plans to market research are set forth. The focus of both subsections is on the effectiveness of market research management and its staff to fulfill its assigned tasks in researching new products. Underlying these questions is the next subsection, which evaluates market research structures for undertaking specific studies. More specifically, questions relating to emerging and shifting markets are asked.

In the leadership subsection, the capabilities of the market research manager are examined. Also, the effectiveness of market research communication from sources outside the group, especially from customers, is evaluated. Similarly, the exchange of ideas between the market research group and its management is examined for determining communication effectiveness. Within the control subsection, market research costs are reviewed to determine the degree of management control over ongoing projects. In most cases, costs are compared to budgeted amounts, which forms the basis for corrective action.

Advertising

The advertising section of the marketing management audit questionnaire (see section IV of Figure 5-1) is an extension of the sales section. An all-inclusive sales plan should include long-range as well as short- to medium-range advertising plans. From that perspective, questions relating to such areas as the adequacy of the advertising budget and the tie-in of regular and special promotions to advertising are evaluated. Next, questions relating to the advertising structure are evaluated. The central focus of this subsection is on the competency of advertising management to meet current sales objectives during upswings and downswings of the economy. The management-by-exception principle is employed to compare actual advertising costs to budgeted amounts. Also, advertising management's ability to integrate its own area with personal selling and promotion is evaluated.

Within the next subsection, advertising leadership is examined from several managerial viewpoints. For instance, is the organization an innovator in advertising, does it keep with the times, and does it have a well-thought-out advertising program? Although it may well be progressive in advertising, its methods of communication must be compatible with the message directed at its customers. In essence, there must be a balance in the overall advertising program to reap its full benefits. Also, there must be adequate managerial control over the advertising effort. In the final subsection, advertising control is therefore evaluated, with the accent on keeping advertising costs within the budgeted amounts.

Physical Distribution

As with the prior sections, the physical distribution (PD) section (see section V of Figure 5-1) of the marketing management audit questionnaire is an integral part of marketing activities. To ensure proper distribution of an organization's products (services), the first subsection of long-range plans centers on questions that are oriented toward the future. Fundamentally, these questions on distribution assess the value received for cost incurred. In the next subsection, the physical distribution structure is evaluated from several viewpoints, namely, their number, their efficiency, and the ability to meet changing conditions.

Within the leadership subsection, distribution channels under PD management are assessed in terms of their ability to move a large volume of merchandise to customers at a low cost and, at the same time, achieve a high rate of inventory turnover. Complementary to this subsection is one on communication. These questions highlight physical distribution effectiveness or lack thereof, particularly in relaying essential managerial and operational information. In the last subsection, physical distribution control is reviewed, particularly in the areas of costs and inventories.

APPLICATION OF MANAGEMENT AUDIT QUESTIONNAIRE TO LONG-RANGE MARKETING PLANS

Recently, the corporate planning staff of the XYZ Company has completed its proposed long-range plans for the next five years. These formalized plans were forwarded to the president for review before they were presented to the board of directors. After a thorough review, the president had one major misgiving about the long-range plans: while programs for new equipment and tooling are projected on a realistic basis, new product development appears to be marginal, that is, it fails to challenge the marketing department. Goals, as set by the planning staff, can be reached without much difficulty. In fact, they are easily obtainable, which disturbs the president.

In view of this fact, the president asked a consultant to the board of directors who is currently employed by a management consulting firm to review the marketing area so as· to detect long-range marketing deficiencies. In addition, the consultant has been asked to supply recommendations that will improve the acceptability of the long-range marketing plans.

Being accustomed to evaluating an organization in part or total via a management audit questionnaire, the consultant completed the long-range planning subsection on sales (see Figure 5-2). After extensive discussions with the marketing vice president and his managers, most questions were answered in the affirmative. However, several no answers point to a lack of progressiveness by marketing executives, thereby providing a working tool for investigating planning weaknesses.

The first question—a very important one—has been answered in the neg-

Figure 5-2. XYZ Company evaluation of long-range sales product development.

	YES	NO	N.A.

SALES

A. Long-Range Plans:

1. Is sales management of sufficient caliber to meet long-range sales objectives? — X —
2. Have sales been adequate over the long run to meet organization objectives? X — —
3. Has the organization maintained its *past* share of the total market? X — —
4. Does the organization have a strategy for maintaining its *future* share of the total market? — X —
5. Do long-range plans include the leveling out of sales peaks and valleys? — X —
6. Are sales forecasting techniques:
   a. used? X — —
   b. adequate? X — —
7. Does the organization calculate long-range data for products by:
   a. sales volumes? X — —
   b. contribution factors? X — —
   c. breakeven points? X — —
8. Are long-range sales quotas established for:
   a. products or product lines? X — —
   b. sales or geographical areas? X — —
   c. salespersons? X — —
9. Are the organization's products or product lines diversified? X — —
10. Does the organization have a policy on developing new products? X — —
11. Is this policy adequate for developing future growth? — X —
12. Is there an adequate long-range program for developing the sales force in the future? X — —
13. Are sales service policies adequate for future growth? X — —
14. Are the organization's products relevant to the times? — X —
15. Does the organization have advantages over its competition in the long run? — X —
16. Are there adequate incentive programs to keep sales at a desired level? X — —
17. Does the sales compensation plan encourage long-range sales as well as immediate sales? X — —

Questionnaire Comments (Negative Answers):

Question 1   Sales management is content to use higher sales prices rather than imagination and initiative to challenge its members to meet specific long-range sales goals.

Question 4   Although sales objectives over the next five years can be met, there will be a weakening of the organization's market share. Fundamentally, sales growth will come from increased sales prices and not from an increased market share.

Question 5   Demand for the company's products is seasonal. However, there is need to smooth production for sales peaks and valleys.

Question 11   The organization's future sales plans are lacking in the development of new products and product lines for emerging markets.

Question 14   While the present products are relevant to the times, future products may not be, because of the reliance on increased selling prices rather than product innovation.

Question 15   Based upon the previous answer, the organization probably will not have an advantage over its competition in the long run. In fact, it looks as if its competition will have an advantage over the company.

---

ative since sales management has lacked the imagination and initiative to develop challenging long-range sales goals. The next two questions have been answered in the affirmative, which indicates a favorable condition. However, the same cannot be said about question 4 relating to future sales performance. Although the answer to question 3 is affirmative, because the company has maintained its *past* share of the total market, question 4 must be answered in the negative. In reality, the firm does not have a strategy for maintaining its *future* share of the total market, but rather is relying heavily upon increased selling prices to enhance profit levels over the long run. Such a condition is a significant weakness in long-range sales planning and must be rectified. Final recommendations to the chief executive officer must include corrective action on this important matter.

The fifth question, which relates to leveling out sales peaks and valleys, is answered negatively, since the demand for the company's consumer products is necessarily somewhat seasonal, peaking especially during the Christmas season. However, recommendations can be made for smoothing production and distribution fluctuations by using specific quantitative methods in the information system.

Questions 6 through 8 received a favorable response. Upon closer inspection, they are but one side of the coin. Although sales forecasting techniques are employed, long-range product data are calculated, and long-range sales quotas are established, their application to sales planning does not seem effective. For example, sales quotas are established by products and product lines for the XYZ Company, but how challenging are these long-range sales quotas? As indicated previously, they are easily obtainable and fail to take into account an increasing total market.

In a similar manner, question 9, which relates to the diversification of the company's products, can be answered with yes, because there are approximately 40 products available for distribution and sale. Continuing with this same line of thought, question 10 asks if the company has a policy for developing new products, and question 11 asks about its adequacy for future growth. The former can be answered in the affirmative, while the latter must receive an unfavorable response. The fact is that even though there is a policy for developing new products for emerging markets, it is inadequate for future growth that is challenging to the marketing department. Thus, certain questions, such as 9 through 11, must be viewed in their totality for a better view of the company's products.

Affirmative answers to questions 12 and 13 may indicate an adequate sales force and effective sales service policies; however, this condition can be changed overnight, as indicated by the answer to question 14. This question highlights the relevance of the company's products to the times. If the organization is content to rely upon increased selling prices rather than product innovation, it has a high chance of reversing its past favorable marketing position. This important point is brought out in the next question, ''Does the organization have advantages over its competition in the long run?'' This question rates a negative answer. In effect, something is lacking in long-range sales plans.

Now that the sales subsection of the marketing management audit questionnaire has been completed, the resulting negative answers provide a starting point for some additional thought-provoking questions. For example, do proposed increases in selling prices fit established long-range plans, or must all or part of the corporate plan be revised to include a new challenging standard of performance? What are the social, ecological, and economic implications of the proposed change? Will the change provide a more marketable substitute for the present products? What impact will the change have on existing strategies, programs, policies, and procedures? How much will the change cost in total dollars? How much will be saved in money or natural resources? Can the change be made at a later time and at what cost? Does the change provide for business fluctuations? What would happen if the change were not undertaken? The foregoing listing is by no means complete, but it is indicative of the type of questions to be asked and answered by the consultant.

Recommendations to Improve Long-Range Marketing Plans

On the basis of an exhaustive study of deficiencies through the marketing management audit questionnaire, the consultant has uncovered the following information. The market which the XYZ Company is serving is experiencing increasing competition, growing out of present product innovation by two competing firms. This competitive condition is expected to increase within the next two years and reach a high point within five years. Further investigation uncovered a significant marketing factor: the trend of manufacturers and distributors to produce specialized products that carry a private label, say for a major retailing or discount chain. Volume is sufficient to warrant production for these large customers. This dichotomy of increasing competition and trend toward private labels, needless to say, will not only have a direct affect on the company's sales function, but also be linked to market research, advertising, and physical distribution. Likewise, other functional areas will be involved.

In view of these important marketing factors, the consultant began work on developing one or more recommendations to the president. Basically, his recommendations must correct the inadequacies of relying upon price increases to keep the organization profitable and viable. To formulate acceptable, convincing recommendations, he must isolate the underlying issues. In very broad terms, this means the following questions must be answered affirmatively:

- Has the actual or real problem been discovered?
- Do the alternatives fit organizational objectives and strategies?
- Do the alternatives fit company resources?
- Do environmental trends and/or company developments challenge the validity of present corporate plans?
- Do proposed alternatives meet the needs for change?
- Are the proposed alternatives practical for the company?
- Will top management be committed to these alternatives?

Affirmative positions on these questions provide a framework for pursuing final recommendations.

After a thorough analysis of the pertinent information, the consultant recommended a new marketing strategy that is complementary to the present one. This strategy involves developing specialized products (private labels) to enhance the company's present product lines. This would take advantage of promising opportunities in producing and distributing specialized products at acceptable profit margins, selling directly to large retailers at lower personal selling costs, reducing warehousing costs through a reduction in the size of company-operated warehouses, and utilizing more fully the talents of the market research as well as the research and development departments.

Such an innovative strategy would include revamping many of the corporate plans, both short- and long-range. Clearly, it is better to take the time now to implement such a change than at some future date; in this manner, the management of the XYZ Company has a better competitive position as the long run becomes the short run.

APPLICATION OF MANAGEMENT AUDIT QUESTIONNAIRE TO MARKET RESEARCH LEADERSHIP

Just recently, the market research manager for the XYZ Company received some rather uncomplimentary remarks from the vice president in charge of marketing. The latter stated that one competitor had just introduced new products that were equal or better in performance, and at the same time lower-priced, than the company's competing products. In view of these new product introductions, the company will not only lose an important part of its established product markets, but also have its image tarnished as leader in introducing new and improved products at savings to its customers. In short, the company's history of aggressiveness in the marketplace has been severely set back within the past few weeks.

Due to the magnitude of the problem, the marketing vice president approached the same consultant who resolved the prior problem and who has a long history of involvement in product development. The consultant feels that an appropriate starting point for analyzing the problem is to utilize a portion of the marketing management audit questionnaire, namely, the market research section (see Figure 5-3). As might be expected, a review of the completed questions indicates several negative answers that need to be analyzed further.

In the opinion of the consultant, the skills of the market research manager are not as current as they should be, as indicated by his answer to the first question. This conclusion is based upon the negative answers to questions 3, 4, and 6. The market research manager fails to require that his subordinates incorporate the dynamics of the marketplace—that is, population shifts and shifts of market potential—in departmental studies. Likewise, he does not exert sufficient influence to get the desired market statistics. Also, the market research manager fails to exert his influence in making computer-oriented statistical market research tools available to his members for more effective analysis of potential products in new and established markets. Overall, the market research manager has taken a traditional approach to market research, ignoring the newer methods of tailoring products to a specific market.

Although not shown in this case study for the XYZ Company, the other subsections on marketing and the entire section on research and development

Figure 5-3. XYZ Company evaluation of market research leadership.

	YES	NO	N.A.
MARKET RESEARCH			

D. Leadership:

1. Is the market research group under the direction of capable and progressive management?

	YES	NO	N.A.
		X	

2. Does market research management make its presence felt in planning:

	YES	NO	N.A.
a. sales quotas?	X		
b. advertising?	X		
c. physical distribution?	X		

3. Does market research management require that the dynamics of the marketplace, i.e., trends to the suburbs, shifts of market potential, be incorporated in market research studies?

	YES	NO	N.A.
		X	

4. Is market research management capable of exerting influence to get desired market statistics regarding characteristics of the population, i.e., income, number in the family, and buying habits?

	YES	NO	N.A.
		X	

5. Is market research management capable of exerting sufficient influence to analyze market areas on the basis of sales potential and desired market shares?

	YES	NO	N.A.
	X		

6. Does market research management exert sufficient influence to make new statistical tools available to its staff?

	YES	NO	N.A.
		X	

Questionnaire Comments (Negative Answers):

Question 1   The skills of the market research manager are too traditional for overseeing today's market research activities.

Question 3   Since the market research manager does not demand the incorporation of market dynamics in their studies, the market research group normally does not include such data. However, some market research studies have included the dynamics of the marketplace.

Question 4   Since the market research manager is oriented toward traditional approaches to studying market behavior, he has not exerted any influence to obtain desired market data.

Question 6   Being traditionally oriented, the market research manager has not spent the necessary time to analyze the applicability of the newer statistical tools for his group.

(see Chapter 6) have been answered to ensure that all major problems relating to new product leadership have been uncovered.

Recommendations to Improve Market Research Leadership

Having completed his questionnaire analysis of the market research department, the consultant had little difficulty in sizing up the situation. Many an organization, like the XYZ Company, fails to establish high performance expectations that elicit results. Many times, managers fail because it requires that they impose certain demands on subordinates. To avoid facing facts, the manager rationalizes that his subordinates are doing the best that can be expected. In a few words, this condition exists in this company, where the market research manager has failed to exert the necessary leadership that will result in higher performance levels from his subordinates.

Key recommendations to the vice president in charge of marketing center on improving the leadership capabilities of the market research manager and upgrading expected results from the company's market researchers. In order to effect these basic recommendations, the consultant has developed the following plan.

First, periodic market research goals will be set for the manager and his subordinates. For market research personnel, this means that market dynamics, market statistics, and certain computerized statistical tools will be an integral part of ongoing market research activities. Second, the market research manager will specify the maximum as well as the minimum expectations for results. These expectations, in turn, will be communicated to all personnel in order to hold them accountable for results. Third, the market research manager will monitor all projects to make sure that specific goals are accomplished on time. Fourth, once success has been achieved on initial project goals, the next projects should lend themselves to a further expansion of market research methods. This last step will lead to an increase in the capabilities of the market research group, which will be alerted to discerning new product opportunities faster. These increasing capabilities of the market research manager and his personnel should assist the XYZ Company in regaining its position as an aggressive product innovator.

Summary

The main thrust of this chapter has been on the presentation of the marketing management audit questionnaire. Specifically, the questionnaire was divided into the following subsections: I. Marketing Overview, II. Sales, III. Market Research, IV. Advertising, and V. Physical Distribution. This breakdown serves to pinpoint those major marketing functions that may not be performing according to predetermined organizational objectives, caused in part or whole by the lack of effective marketing management.

Additionally, this chapter has highlighted the application of this questionnaire to selected marketing problems—long-range marketing plans and market research leadership. As demonstrated in these case studies, the questionnaire provides a starting point for making appropriate recommendations to eliminate managerial and operational deficiencies.

6

Evaluating Research & Development and Engineering

EVALUATION OF RESEARCH & DEVELOPMENT and engineering by utilizing a management audit questionnaire complements the analysis of marketing, in particular, market research. The importance of research & development to a company's growth cannot be overstated. A productive research & development effort is a prime source of new products and processes crucial to the company in the long run. Once new products have been developed to a certain stage, the engineering department takes over the detailed design and testing. This phase includes value engineering (value analysis) for controlling costs of the new product. Likewise, the engineering function is concerned with implementing manufacturing facilities that are capable of producing the product at the lowest cost. Thus, marketing and research & development, combined with engineering, provide the necessary thrust for meeting anticipated customer and market needs now and in the future.

Within this chapter, the following sections of the research and development and engineering management audit questionnaire (see Figure 6-1) are presented:

I. Research & Development and Engineering Overview
II. Research & Development
III. Engineering

(text continues on page 127)

**Figure 6-1. Management Audit Questionnaire:
Research & Development and Engineering.**

	YES	NO	N.A.

I. RESEARCH & DEVELOPMENT AND
   ENGINEERING OVERVIEW

A. Long-Range Plans:

 1. Are long-range R&D and engineering
    plans in agreement with:
    a. long-range organization objectives? ___ ___ ___
    b. long-range plans of other functional
       areas? ___ ___ ___
    c. medium-range R&D and engineering
       plans? ___ ___ ___
    d. short-range R&D and engineering
       plans? ___ ___ ___
 2. Are long-range R&D and engineering
    plans reviewed by:
    a. board of directors? ___ ___ ___
    b. top management? ___ ___ ___
 3. Is there an official planning committee
    to develop long-range R&D and engi-
    neering plans? ___ ___ ___
 4. Does R&D and engineering manage-
    ment accept and understand these
    long-range plans? ___ ___ ___
 5. Are R&D and engineering efforts
    directed toward accomplishing these
    long-range plans? ___ ___ ___
 6. Is performance against long-range R&D
    and engineering plans measured peri-
    odically? ___ ___ ___
 7. Are long-range R&D and engineering
    plans reviewed periodically so as to stay
    current? ___ ___ ___
 8. Is the management by exception princi-
    ple an integral part of long-range R&D
    and engineering plans? ___ ___ ___

B. Short-Range Plans:

 1. Are short- or medium-range R&D and
    engineering plans in agreement with:
    a. short- or medium-range organization
       objectives? ___ ___ ___
    b. short- or medium-range plans of
       other functional areas? ___ ___ ___
    c. long-range R&D and engineering
       plans? ___ ___ ___

	YES	NO	N.A.

2. Are short- or medium-range R&D and engineering plans reviewed by:
   a. top management? ___ ___ ___
   b. middle management? ___ ___ ___
   c. lower management? ___ ___ ___
3. Are there procedures for developing short- or medium-range R&D and engineering plans? ___ ___ ___
4. Does R&D and engineering management accept and understand these short- or medium-range plans? ___ ___ ___
5. Are R&D and engineering management efforts directed toward accomplishing these short- or medium-range plans? ___ ___ ___
6. Is performance against short- or medium-range plans measured periodically? ___ ___ ___
7. Are short- or medium-range R&D and engineering plans reviewed periodically to stay current? ___ ___ ___
8. Is the management by exception principle an integral part of short- or medium-range R&D and engineering plans? ___ ___ ___

C. Organization Structure:

1. Are the R&D and engineering organization charts compatible with other functional organization charts? ___ ___ ___
2. Is it clear who is charged with responsibility and who has authority over:
   a. pure research? ___ ___ ___
   b. applied research (where the focus is on product development)? ___ ___ ___
   c. product design? ___ ___ ___
   d. plant engineering? ___ ___ ___
3. Does each person in R&D and engineering know his or her job well? ___ ___ ___
4. Is it clear what the superior–subordinate relationships are in the R&D and engineering departments? ___ ___ ___
5. Are there adequate job descriptions for each R&D and engineering position? ___ ___ ___
6. Is there a competent employee assigned to each R&D and engineering position? ___ ___ ___
7. Is the level of R&D and engineering training adequate for:
   a. management? ___ ___ ___
   b. employees? ___ ___ ___

	YES	NO	N.A.

8. Can the quality of R&D and engineering personnel be assessed for:
   a. management?
   b. employees?
9. Are the R&D and engineering departments adequately staffed?
10. Are reporting requirements clearly defined and understood by R&D and engineering personnel?
11. Are R&D and engineering management held accountable for their actions?
12. Are there provisions within the R&D and engineering departments for periodic review of their organization structure?

D. Leadership:

1. Does research & development management provide the leadership to accomplish desired goals that are in harmony with overall company objectives?
2. Does engineering management provide the leadership to accomplish its stated objectives?
3. Does R&D and engineering management keep itself and its personnel abreast of competitive developments?
4. Does R&D and engineering management provide the necessary leadership to effect rapid changes in ongoing programs and projects as the need arises?
5. Does R&D and engineering management make constructive use of ideas and suggestions from its personnel in its ongoing programs and projects?
6. Does R&D and engineering management provide an open atmosphere with a high degree of confidence and trust so that favorable results are obtainable from ongoing programs and projects?

E. Communication:

1. Are communication channels adequate to facilitate the accomplishment of R&D and engineering goals?
2. Is there adequate communication between research & development and:

	YES	NO	N.A.
a. market research?	___	___	___
b. engineering?	___	___	___
c. accounting?	___	___	___

3. Is there adequate communication between engineering and:
   a. market research? ___ ___ ___
   b. research & development? ___ ___ ___
   c. accounting? ___ ___ ___
4. Do R&D and engineering personnel feel free to communicate problems related to their programs or projects to their superiors? ___ ___ ___
5. Are the accomplishments of R&D and engineering personnel made known to people:
   a. within the company? ___ ___ ___
   b. outside the company? ___ ___ ___
6. Are R&D and engineering personnel informed of competitive developments and the resulting impact on their programs and projects? ___ ___ ___
7. Is there an effective communication system that feeds important research information to R&D and engineering personnel for integration within their programs and projects? ___ ___ ___
8. Does management have adequate feedback on the progress and costs of ongoing R&D and engineering programs and projects? ___ ___ ___

F. Control:

1. Is there control over R&D and engineering objectives to ensure that they are in harmony with overall company objectives? ___ ___ ___
2. Are effective control reports, methods, and techniques used in:
   a. research & development? ___ ___ ___
   b. engineering? ___ ___ ___
3. Is close control maintained over research and engineering costs? ___ ___ ___
4. Are projects adequately controlled as they move from the R&D phase to the engineering phase? ___ ___ ___
5. Are research & development goals periodically compared to actual results (budget versus actual)? ___ ___ ___

	YES	NO	N.A.

6. Are engineering goals periodically compared to actual results (budget versus actual)? ___ ___ ___

II. RESEARCH & DEVELOPMENT ___ ___ ___

A. Long-Range Plans:

1. Are R&D projects in conformity with company objectives? ___ ___ ___
2. Is R&D management of sufficient caliber to meet long-range research and development objectives? ___ ___ ___
3. Is there a long-range research program for developing new:
   a. products? ___ ___ ___
   b. manufacturing processes? ___ ___ ___
   c. manufacturing equipment? ___ ___ ___
4. Does the company have an ongoing program to improve existing:
   a. products? ___ ___ ___
   b. manufacturing processes? ___ ___ ___
   c. manufacturing equipment? ___ ___ ___
5. Are the long-range efforts of R&D coordinated with market research? ___ ___ ___
6. Is planning used for long-range R&D programs? ___ ___ ___
7. Are R&D facilities adequate for long-range projects? ___ ___ ___
8. Is the R&D budget adequate to accomplish company long-range plans? ___ ___ ___
9. Are there enough applied R&D projects being undertaken to produce the desired sales volume in future years? ___ ___ ___
10. Is the R&D department geared to make rapid changes in its projects? ___ ___ ___
11. Does the company spend an average amount for R&D activities in comparison with its competition? ___ ___ ___
12. Are high-level R&D personnel attracted by the company? ___ ___ ___
13. Are company R&D personnel attracted by:
    a. working conditions? ___ ___ ___
    b. patent policies (that is, are they encouraged to develop patents)? ___ ___ ___
    c. publication policies (that is, are they encouraged to publish)? ___ ___ ___
    d. high salaries? ___ ___ ___

	YES	NO	N.A.

B. Short- or Medium-Range Plans:

1. Is research and development management of sufficient caliber to meet short- or medium-range R&D plans? — — —
2. Is planning of R&D projects accomplished by some type of systematic procedures? — — —
3. Are R&D data on new product developments forwarded to market research? — — —
4. Are R&D programs flexible enough to accommodate changes in the short run? — — —
5. Are current sales the result of product innovation and improvement from R&D programs? — — —
6. Do short- or medium-range R&D programs generate sufficient new and improved products to yield satisfactory profits? — — —
7. Are mathematical/statistical techniques employed in R&D projects? — — —

C. Organization Structure:

1. Is the research & development department under the direction of a qualified manager? — — —
2. Does the organization structure lend itself to the development of new product ideas? — — —
3. Are current R&D projects organized toward accomplishing effective results? — — —
4. Does the R&D structure lend itself to making rapid changes in its programs? — — —
5. Does the R&D structure lend itself to attracting high-caliber personnel? — — —
6. Are R&D facilities adequate to accomplish the desired results? — — —
7. In the development of new products, has proper consideration been given to:
   a. manufacturing capacity? — — —
   b. trial runs? — — —
   c. economy in manufacturing? — — —

D. Leadership:

1. Is the research & development manager a leader in the sense that he or she exerts the necessary leadership to accomplish established R&D objectives and predetermined project deadlines? — — —

YES   NO   N.A.

2. Does R&D management speak out on its behalf for sufficient funding so as to be at least comparable to its competitors?   ___   ___   ___

3. Does the R&D group stand out as a leader in its field so as to attract promising personnel?   ___   ___   ___

4. Is there a high degree of teamwork in ongoing research programs and projects?   ___   ___   ___

5. Does R&D management keep abreast of its industry's new developments and its customer requirements for new products/services?   ___   ___   ___

6. Do R&D personnel have a real responsibility for their programs and projects and behave in a constructive way to undertake them?   ___   ___   ___

7. Are R&D personnel sufficiently motivated by R&D management to become fully involved in their work and all decisions relating to it?   ___   ___   ___

8. Do R&D personnel feel free to discuss all types of matters—problems, instructions, etc.—with their superiors?   ___   ___   ___

E. Communication:

1. Does market research communicate the specifics of new product development adequately to R&D personnel?   ___   ___   ___

2. Are *downward* and *upward* communication channels used effectively to keep R&D personnel abreast of pertinent research developments?   ___   ___   ___

3. Do R&D personnel keep abreast of the changing technology in terms of:
   a. new quantitative tools for developing new products?   ___   ___   ___
   b. new testing methods?   ___   ___   ___
   c. new and simpler manufacturing processes?   ___   ___   ___

4. Are major R&D developments of competition as well as noncompeting firms transmitted to company R&D personnel?   ___   ___   ___

5. Are important R&D publications, i.e., books, articles, and speeches, forwarded to and read by appropriate R&D personnel?   ___   ___   ___

	YES	NO	N.A.

F. <u>Control</u>:

1. Is close control exercised by the R&D manager over research projects?

2. Is control over R&D projects accomplished by some type of systematic approach, such as Gantt charts and PERT networks?

3. Does the R&D group keep abreast of:
   a. customer requirements?
   b. new developments?
   c. competitive developments?

4. Does the R&D manager exercise sufficient control over his or her personnel to accomplish the desired results?

5. Does the R&D manager encourage his or her personnel to utilize appropriate research methods and techniques to effect better control over their projects?

6. Does the R&D manager exercise sufficient control so that research and development projects are kept within reasonable limits, that is, will value be received for cost incurred?

7. Are R&D project estimates compared to actual results so that corrective action can be undertaken if results are below expectations?

III. ENGINEERING

A. <u>Long-Range Plans</u>:

1. Is the engineering department fulfilling organization objectives?

2. Is engineering management of sufficient caliber to meet long-range engineering objectives?

3. Is value analysis (value engineering) emphasized in developing new products so as to minimize costs?

4. In the engineering of new products over the years, has proper consideration been given to:
   a. manufacturing processes?
   b. product quality?
   c. trial runs to avoid "bugs" in the manufacturing process?
   d. standardization of equipment?
   e. simplification of the manufacturing process?

YES   NO   N.A.

    f. establishment of quality control points in the manufacturing process?   ____ ____ ____

    g. minimization of labor requirements during manufacture?   ____ ____ ____

    h. minimization of maintenance of manufacturing equipment?   ____ ____ ____

5. Are planning methods exercised over long-range engineering projects?   ____ ____ ____

6. Are engineering facilities adequate to accomplish long-range projects?   ____ ____ ____

7. Is the engineering budget adequate to attain long-range goals?   ____ ____ ____

8. Does the company spend an average sum for engineering in comparison with competition?   ____ ____ ____

9. Is the engineering department flexible enough to make rapid changes in its projects?   ____ ____ ____

B. Short- or Medium-Range Plans:

1. Is engineering management of sufficient caliber to meet short- or medium-range engineering objectives?   ____ ____ ____

2. Are there short- or medium-range engineering plans?   ____ ____ ____

3. Do short- or medium-range plans give the engineering department sufficient time to design new and improved products so as to incorporate value analysis (value engineering)?   ____ ____ ____

4. Do short- or medium-range plans provide for unforeseen engineering contingencies?   ____ ____ ____

5. Are mathematical or statistical methods employed in the engineering design process where deemed necessary?   ____ ____ ____

C. Organization Structure:

1. Is the engineering department under the direction of a qualified manager?   ____ ____ ____

2. Is there a logical structure to the engineering department?   ____ ____ ____

3. Is the organization structure flexible enough for making rapid changes in engineering programs and projects?   ____ ____ ____

4. Is the engineering environment such that it can employ computerized procedures when designing a new product?   ____ ____ ____

	YES	NO	N.A.

5. Does the engineering structure lend itself to attracting high-caliber personnel? ___ ___ ___
6. Are engineering facilities organized to accomplish the desired results? ___ ___ ___
7. In the design of new products, has proper consideration been given to:
   a. standardization of materials? ___ ___ ___
   b. minimum labor content? ___ ___ ___
   c. product quality? ___ ___ ___
   d. standardization of equipment? ___ ___ ___

D. Leadership:

1. Is the engineering department manager a leader, that is, does he or she exert the required leadership to accomplish established engineering objectives and project deadlines? ___ ___ ___
2. Is engineering management sufficiently progressive to obtain the necessary facilities that are needed to accomplish the results expected? ___ ___ ___
3. Does engineering management provide the necessary leadership to get its share of company funds? ___ ___ ___
4. Does engineering management exhibit leadership by:
   a. improving product quality with a resulting reduction in cost? ___ ___ ___
   b. increasing standardization of materials? ___ ___ ___
   c. improving manufacturing methods and processes through simplification? ___ ___ ___
   d. decreasing labor requirements with a resulting reduction in cost? ___ ___ ___
5. Do engineering supervisors have confidence and trust in their subordinates? ___ ___ ___
6. Do engineering personnel exhibit a high degree of cooperation in their programs and projects? ___ ___ ___
7. Are engineering personnel involved in decisions that affect their own programs and projects? ___ ___ ___

E. Communication:

1. Are *downward* and *upward* communication channels used effectively to keep engineering personnel abreast of pertinent engineering developments? ___ ___ ___

YES   NO   N.A.

2. Do R&D personnel specify the requirements of new products in sufficient detail for engineering personnel?   ___ ___ ___

3. Are current costs of basic raw materials
   furnished by purchasing to engineering
   personnel in order to keep new product
   costs at a minimum, that is, is "value
   engineering" practiced?   ___ ___ ___

4. Are the positive effects of standardization of materials and processes
   transmitted periodically to all engineering personnel?   ___ ___ ___

5. Are lower-cost manufacturing methods
   developed and communicated to production personnel?   ___ ___ ___

6. Are bills of materials updated to reflect
   current engineering changes?   ___ ___ ___

7. Are changed bills of materials sent to
   the production department?   ___ ___ ___

F. Control:

1. Does the engineering manager exercise
   sufficient control over engineering programs and projects?   ___ ___ ___

2. Does the engineering manager exercise
   sufficient control to make rapid
   changes in engineering programs and
   projects?   ___ ___ ___

3. Does the engineering manager encourage his or her personnel to utilize appropriate engineering methods and
   techniques to effect better control over
   their programs and projects?   ___ ___ ___

4. Does the engineering manager exercise
   sufficient control over engineering programs and projects to effect:
   a. standardization of materials?   ___ ___ ___
   b. standardization of equipment?   ___ ___ ___
   c. simplification of manufacturing pro-
      cesses?   ___ ___ ___
   d. economy in manufacturing?   ___ ___ ___

5. Has the engineering manager sufficient
   control over his or her personnel to prevent current programs and projects
   from being overengineered, that is, to
   avoid high engineering costs with little
   or no value received?   ___ ___ ___

6. Are bills of materials specifications updated in accordance with the latest engineering revisions?   ___ ___ ___

	YES	NO	N.A.
7. Are manufacturing process sheets updated in accordance with the latest engineering revisions?	—	—	—
8. Are engineering program and project estimates compared to actual results so that corrective action can be undertaken if results are below expectations?	—	—	—

Due to the comprehensive nature of the questions, these sections of the questionnaire are capable of pinpointing R&D and engineering problems that are caused by managerial and operational deficiencies.

The presentation of the questionnaire is followed by two sample applications for the XYZ Company. These applications will focus on research and development plans and engineering control.

COMMENTS ON THE R&D AND ENGINEERING QUESTIONNAIRE

Research & Development and Engineering Overview

The flow of information about new products and processes from market research, customers, and other sources provides the impetus for starting specific research & development projects. In turn, the results of these R&D projects are the basis for engineering new products and processes for a company. The interplay among these areas does not stop with engineering; rather, engineering serves as a connecting link to manufacturing operations. Hence, an overview of research & development and engineering must take into account not only the effectiveness of the information flow from one area to another, but also the capabilities of management to coordinate its activities in an ever-changing business environment.

The principal purpose of this initial section of the questionnaire is to evaluate the capability of R&D and engineering management to cope with changing conditions. Also, the proper meshing of these two functions with other functional areas is assessed to help the evaluator in determining the degree of accomplishment of predetermined organization objectives.

Research and Development

After market research has ascertained the feasibility of bringing a new product to the marketplace, it is the function of research and development to develop the product up to a point where engineering can take over the detailed design and testing. This developmental phase is called *applied* research, as opposed to *pure* research, where no particular end product is in mind.

In the first two subsections of the research and development section, questions on long-range and short- to medium-range R&D plans are set forth. In both subsections, the effectiveness of research and development management and its staff in fulfilling their assigned tasks is evaluated. Underlying these areas is the next subsection, which examines the suitability of the R&D organization structure for undertaking specific research studies.

Within the next subsection, the ability of R&D management to exert the necessary leadership to accomplish stated objectives and oversee R&D projects effectively is examined. In a somewhat similar manner, the upward and downward flows of information between research & development management and its staff are assessed for determining the effectiveness of communication. In the last subsection, questions relating to the degree of management control over ongoing R&D projects are reviewed. Great accent is placed not only on comparing actual results with planned results, but also on providing for corrective action if results are below expectations.

Engineering

As indicated previously, the engineering department takes over from the research efforts of the R&D department. Specifically, engineering must design and test the product before it can be manufactured. Engineering blueprints must be drawn and distributed to the appropriate manufacturing and purchasing departments. Sometimes, special manufacturing processes and methods must be designed before manufacturing operations can commence.

The first subsection of the engineering section of the management audit questionnaire looks at long-range planning while the second subsection reviews short- to medium-range plans. Both are concerned with the effectiveness of engineering management in fulfilling its assigned duties and responsibilities. Special emphasis is placed on value engineering, or value analysis, in developing new products at minimum cost. An integral part of these short- to long-range engineering plans is the organization structure that permits these plans to be carried out in an efficient and economical manner.

In the leadership subsection, engineering management is examined in terms of its ability to lead its staff to accomplish its objectives as well as program and project deadlines. Similarly, the exchange of ideas among engineering management and its staff is evaluated so as to determine the effec-

EVALUATING RESEARCH & DEVELOPMENT AND ENGINEERING   129

tiveness of downward and upward channels of communication. In the last
subsection, engineering control over ongoing projects is reviewed for adequacy. In cases where actual results have exceeded budgeted costs, there
should be a mechanism for corrective action.

APPLICATION OF MANAGEMENT AUDIT QUESTIONNAIRE TO RESEARCH & DEVELOPMENT PLANS

One of the problems that the marketing questionnaire indicated (see Chapter
5) was the lack of a strategy for maintaining or increasing the XYZ Company's share of the market. A strategy of this nature involves many functional areas. The following facts are useful in understanding this problem.

The research & development department is headed by Dr. Robert A.
Morgan, a long-term employee who was once described by the president of
the XYZ Company as the most valuable man in the organization. This statement was made 25 years ago—at the time Dr. Morgan applied for his fourth
and last patent. At that time, the department was comprised of Dr. Morgan,
three lab assistants, and a secretary. These people worked together and con-
stituted the entire department from 1945 to 1964.

In 1965, the department began to expand. This expansion took place
under the watchful eye of Dr. Morgan, who insisted that he be involved in
every detail of the research that was carried out. He personaly interviewed
everyone hired, made all project assignments, reviewed the weekly progress
reports that he required of each scientist, decided upon all methodology, and
determined whether the results of the research were worth passing on to the
corporate executives for further development. Most of the research to date
has been an extension of the work that Dr. Morgan performed toward the
development of his four patent applications. This work was Morgan's chief
area of interest and had been since his graduate school days in Europe.

In view of the foregoing facts, the board consultant who solved the marketing problems was asked by the president to review the situation and to
make recommendations that would improve the effectiveness of long-range
R&D planning. To undertake this inquiry, the consultant completed the
long-range planning subsection on research and development (see Figure 6-
2). As noted in this subsection of the questionnaire, there are several negative answers that point to the lack of progressiveness on the part of Dr.
Morgan.

The first three questions have been answered negatively, since there is
no formalized long-range planning in conformity with company objectives,
no R&D management capable of meeting long-range research and develop-

Figure 6-2. XYZ Company evaluation of long-range R&D planning.

	YES	NO	N.A.
RESEARCH & DEVELOPMENT			
A. Long-Range Plans:			
1. Are R&D projects in conformity with company objectives?		X	
2. Is R&D management of sufficient caliber to meet long-range research and development objectives?		X	
3. Is there a long-range research program for developing new:			
a. products?		X	
b. manufacturing processes?		X	
c. manufacturing equipment?		X	
4. Does the company have an ongoing program to improve existing:			
a. products?	X		
b. manufacturing processes?	X		
c. manufacturing equipment?	X		
5. Are the long-range efforts of R&D coordinated with market research?		X	
6. Is planning used for long-range R&D programs?		X	
7. Are R&D facilities adequate for long-range projects?	X		
8. Is the R&D budget adequate to accomplish company long-range plans?	X		
9. Are there enough applied R&D projects being undertaken to produce the desired sales volume in future years?		X	
10. Is the R&D department geared to make rapid changes in its projects?		X	
11. Does the company spend an average amount for R&D activities in comparison with its competition?	X		
12. Are high-level R&D personnel attracted by the company?		X	
13. Are company R&D personnel attracted by:			
a. working conditions?			X
b. patent policies?			X
c. publication policies?			X
d. high salaries?			X

Questionnaire Comments (Negative Answers):
Question 1   Since there is no formalized long-range planning policy, Dr. Morgan pursues those projects which he feels are important, as he has in the past.

Question 2	Fundamentally, Dr. Morgan is a technician and not a manager.
Question 3	There is no long-range program for the development of products, processes, and equipment except where they happen to tie in with the interests of Dr. Morgan.
Question 5	By and large, R&D long-range efforts are not coordinated with market research.
Question 6	Because of the close control exercised over R&D projects by Dr. Morgan, formalized planning is not used.
Question 9	Since R&D work centers around existing products and processes, an increase in sales volume would have to come by obtaining a larger share of the market.
Question 10	Rapid changes in R&D projects have never been made. Dr. Morgan is known for his methodical research; changes upset him.
Question 12	Most researchers desire more freedom than Dr. Morgan allows his staff; consequently, they do not stay long.

ment objectives, and no long-range planning program for the development of *new* products, except where they tie in with the interests of Dr. Morgan. However, it should be noted (see question 4) that the company does have an ongoing program to improve *existing* products.

Questions 5 and 6 have been answered negatively. Fundamentally, R&D long-range efforts are not coordinated with market research, and formal planning is not used for long-range R&D programs and projects because of the close control by Dr. Morgan. The next two questions (7 and 8) have been answered in the affirmative and are indicative of the adequacy of R&D facilities and budgets to accomplish long-range plans.

The ninth question, which relates to the adequacy of R&D programs and projects to produce the desired sales volume in future years, is assessed with a negative answer, since R&D work centers around existing products. This same problem was alluded to in question 3 above. A negative answer to the tenth question indicates the non-flexibility of the R&D department, or its inability to meet changing conditions. The reason is that changes upset Dr. Morgan. The last negative answer is found in question 12. High-level researchers are not attracted to the company, since they desire more freedom than Dr. Morgan will allow. Consequently, competent personnel do not stay long.

In addition to answering the questions found in the long-range plans subsection, the other subsections on research & development have been answered to ensure that all major problems pertaining to R&D have been examined. In this manner, the board consultant for the XYZ Company can make definite recommendations on R&D planning to the president.

Recommendations to Improve Research & Development Plans

On the basis of the foregoing R&D review, the board consultant for the XYZ Company needed little time to pinpoint ongoing deficiencies of research & development planning. The key to the case is the first questionnaire question, which was answered negatively. If R&D projects are not in conformity with company objectives, whose objectives are being pursued? It should have been apparent that Dr. Morgan is pursuing his own personal objectives. Perhaps he is simply duplicating on a department level the behavior that made him "the most valuable man in the organization" 25 years ago. Regardless of the reason, this preoccupation has resulted in negative responses for many questions in the questionnaire.

As indicated by the negative answers, R&D efforts are not coordinated with market research, nor are planning methods used. The fact that R&D efforts are so firmly locked in the "glories of the past" also explains the other negative responses. For example, Dr. Morgan's autocratic management style and insistence upon close control give a clue as to why top research personnel are not attracted to the XYZ Company.

Quite often, it is difficult for a company's president to detect the root cause of the difficulties described. The reason is that from a technical point of view, Dr. Morgan is probably as competent, if not more competent, than he ever was. What has happened is that his job has changed. It has changed so subtly that the new nature of the job is not apparent to Dr. Morgan, nor to those above him. In the early days of the department, Dr. Morgan was undoubtedly far more knowledgeable than anyone in the department. He derived a great deal of stature and, hence, power from his expertise. His autocratic manner worked because he knew all the answers; all he asked was rigorous attention to his orders. What is demanded today is managerial expertise, that is, the coordination of many technically competent contributors.

To overcome the foregoing deficiencies of the R&D department, key recommendations are that Dr. Morgan be removed from his position and that an effective R&D administrator be placed in charge immediately. Additionally, Dr. Morgan should be given a title befitting of his past contributions with no cut in pay. He should be given the opportunity to undertake an R&D project that will benefit the company, specifically, the development of one or more new products. In this manner, his talents can be utilized to their fullest. It is highly recommended that the R&D project be directed away from his four patent applications so that he has a chance to take off his "blinders" and explore new territories that will be beneficial to the company in terms of new product development.

APPLICATION OF MANAGEMENT AUDIT QUESTIONNAIRE TO ENGINEERING CONTROL

Fred Gordon, age 37, is an aspiring engineering manager of proven technical ability. He joined the engineering department of the XYZ Company five years ago. Recently, he was named head of the mechanical design group. In this new position, a group of eight engineers are under his direction. At an introductory meeting, it was apparent from his remarks that he was a "driver" who knew exactly what he wanted. He came through to his staff as a hard-working, conscientious supervisor who understood not only technical principles, but also the smallest detail of his speciality.

The first few weeks on the job did not serve to change this initial impression. It was said that when he attended his first managers' conference, he looked at a design under consideration and openly asked, "What stupid person designed this?" This embarrassing situation was alleviated when those present suggested that Gordon's group be given two weeks to improve the design. Gordon, motivated by the challenge, left the meeting determined to undertake the engineering work himself. Within two weeks, his work had been completed. It was generally agreed by his fellow engineers that he had created a superior product; in fact, the engineering managerial committee attested to its improvement over the original.

In the day-to-day operation of his department, Gordon relied upon two men, Chuck Davis and Robert Holmes. As Gordon "cracked the whip," Chuck and Bob carried out the orders. The reaction of the other engineers to his managerial style ranged from nonresistance to open hostility.

The following incident caused many of the nonresistant to join the openly hostile group. Chuck had been put in charge of a field test unit. Apparently, he had misinterpreted Gordon's instructions. (It should be noted that Chuck had been working 23 hours straight prior to his conversation with Gordon.) The test was aborted, and the damage caused by the unsuccessful venture amounted to several thousand dollars, not to mention the time delay to replace critical parts. A group of Gordon's engineers were standing around, weary from another night session, when Gordon "tore" into Chuck. What followed, needless to say, was very embarrassing. The ruthlessness of the verbal attack was matched only by the defenseless subjugation of its target. An associate came to Chuck's defense only to be told that "it was none of his business." It was tacitly understood that if this could happen to Chuck, the fate of a "lesser dignitary" could fairly well be predicted.

Despite these difficulties, the weeks of frantic effort paid off; schedules were met and sometimes improved. The reputation of the department for performance flourished. If credit for success were to be apportioned, Gordon's share would undoubtedly and justifiably be great. He decided not only every major issue, but most minor ones as well. Every drawing was reviewed by him personally. He was there evenings, Sundays, or whenever the work demanded it. He radiated a "can do" attitude. Gordon's performance had not gone unnoticed by top management, which was seriously considering promoting him to chief engineer of all groups. This move would bring 25 engineers and draftsmen under his control.

Taking into account the foregoing factors, the vice president of the research & development and engineering departments had to make a decision regarding Gordon's promotion. To get an objective viewpoint, he turned to an old-time friend who is an engineering consultant. The engineering consultant has decided to use the control subsection of the management audit questionnaire (see Figure 6-3).

The completed subsection on control discloses that all questions have been answered in the affirmative, except for question 5. Although Mr. Gordon has control over his personnel, this control is viewed negatively, since his engineers are spending their time and effort not in trying to be right, but in attempting to keep from being wrong. That is, there is too much emphasis on being safe in a decision, since one cannot afford to make mistakes.

Recommendations to Improve Engineering Control

Based upon the foregoing analysis by the engineering consultant, the problem was not difficult to identify. Briefly, it revolved around the issue of "working with and through people." For the most part, the effect that control can have upon people when it is personalized rather than systematic is demonstrated. Not only is Gordon working night and day, but, more important, his subordinates are afraid to innovate. However, in terms of the pragmatic criteria generally used, Gordon is doing an excellent job.

The pivotal recommendation to the vice president in charge of R&D and engineering concerns the promotion or nonpromotion of Mr. Gordon. In view of the foregoing facts, Mr. Gordon should be promoted only if he undergoes an intensive course in human relations. Human relations training should be away from the XYZ Company for several weeks so that Gordon's deficiencies of working with and through people can be pointed out to him. Also, sufficient time should be accorded to him so that he can change his personal attitudes and feelings in areas observed in this study and learn new human relations approaches. Unless ample time is spent on this much-needed human relations training, the company and its engineering personnel

Figure 6-3. XYZ Company evaluation of engineering controls.

	YES	NO	N.A.

ENGINEERING

F. Control:

1. Does the engineering manager exercise sufficient control over engineering programs and projects? — **X**

2. Does the engineering manager exercise sufficient control to make rapid changes in engineering programs and projects? — **X**

3. Does the engineering manager encourage his or her personnel to utilize appropriate engineering methods and techniques to effect better control over their programs and projects? — **X**

4. Does the engineering manager exercise sufficient control over engineering programs and projects to effect:
   a. standardization of materials? — **X**
   b. standardization of equipment? — **X**
   c. simplification of manufacturing processes? — **X**
   d. economy in manufacturing? — **X**

5. Has the engineering manager sufficient control over his or her personnel to prevent current programs and projects from being overengineered, that is, to avoid high engineering costs with little or no value received? — — **X**

6. Are bills of materials specifications updated in accordance with the latest engineering revisions? — **X**

7. Are manufacturing process sheets updated in accordance with the latest engineering revisions? — **X**

8. Are engineering program and project estimates compared to actual results so that corrective action can be undertaken if results are below expectations? — **X**

Questionnaire Comment (Negative Answer):

Question 5 Because of Gordon's leadership style, most engineers are spending their efforts not in trying to be right, but in attempting to keep from being *wrong*. A feel for this concern can be gathered from the following quote with which a project manager cautioned his people: "Fellows, you got to be safe in your decision. We can't afford to make mistakes, not even little ones which could serve as ammunition for any opposition that might use it for its own purposes. It's like getting into the water when you're not sure of the depth. Slowly, one foot at a time, so as not to slip on your. . . ."

will suffer in the months and years to come from Gordon's narrow view of what constitutes an engineering manager's job.

SUMMARY

The research & development and engineering part of the management audit questionnaire has been the main focus of this chapter. More specifically, the questionnaire was divided into the following sections: I. Research & Development and Engineering Overview, II. Research & Development, and III. Engineering. This breakdown serves to pinpoint R&D and engineering areas that may not be functioning in a manner commensurate with predetermined organizational objectives.

Also in this chapter, two applications of selected subsections of the R&D and engineering management audit questionnaire were presented. These focused on research and development plans and on engineering control. As usual, appropriate recommendations were made to eliminate current managerial and operational problems confronting management.

IV

MANAGEMENT AUDITING

of
Production-Oriented
and Personnel
Functional Areas

7

Evaluating
the Manufacturing
Function

EVALUATION OF THE MANUFACTURING FUNCTION through the management audit questionnaire tends to be complex for most industrial organizations, since the manufacture of finished products usually involves many operations. Not only must plant, equipment, and tools be provided in the manufacturing process, but appropriate personnel must also be hired and trained to utilize the manufacturing facilities. Raw materials and goods in process must be available when needed. Production must be planned, scheduled, routed, and controlled for producing the desired finished goods that meet specific customer deadlines. Hence, a management audit questionnaire in this area must be comprehensive to pinpoint any ongoing managerial and operational deficiencies.

For a complete evaluation of the manufacturing function, the following sections of the manufacturing management audit questionnaire (see Figure 7-1) are set forth:

    I. Manufacturing Overview
   II. Production Planning
  III. Production
  IV. Inventory
   V. Purchasing

From this broad viewpoint, the questionnaire will highlight important manufacturing problems confronting the organization.

As with previous chapters, two sample applications employing specific

(text continues on page 159)

Figure 7-1. Management Audit Questionnaire: Manufacturing.

	YES	NO	N.A.

I. MANUFACTURING OVERVIEW

   A. Long-Range Plans:

      1. Are long-range manufacturing plans in agreement with:

         a. long-range organization objectives?   ____ ____ ____

         b. long-range plans of other functional areas?   ____ ____ ____

         c. medium-range manufacturing plans?

         d. short-range manufacturing plans?   ____ ____ ____

      2. Are long-range manufacturing plans reviewed by:

         a. the board of directors?   ____ ____ ____

         b. top management?   ____ ____ ____

      3. Do long-range manufacturing plans include the following functional areas:

         a. production planning?   ____ ____ ____

         b. production?   ____ ____ ____

         c. inventory?   ____ ____ ____

         d. purchasing?   ____ ____ ____

      4. Is there an official planning committee to develop the long-range manufacturing plans?   ____ ____ ____

      5. Does manufacturing management accept and understand these long-range plans?   ____ ____ ____

      6. Are manufacturing management efforts directed toward accomplishing these long-range plans?   ____ ____ ____

      7. Is performance against long-range manufacturing plans measured periodically?   ____ ____ ____

      8. Are long-range manufacturing plans reviewed periodically so as to stay current?   ____ ____ ____

      9. Is the management by exception principle an integral part of long-range manufacturing plans?   ____ ____ ____

   B. Short- or Medium-Range Plans:

      1. Are short- or medium-range manufacturing plans in agreement with:

         a. short- or medium-range organization objectives?   ____ ____ ____

         b. short- or medium-range plans of other functional areas?   ____ ____ ____

         c. long-range manufacturing plans?   ____ ____ ____

	YES	NO	N.A.

2. Are short- or medium-range manufacturing plans reviewed by:
   a. top management?
   b. middle management?
   c. lower management?
3. Do short- or medium-range manufacturing plans include the following functional areas:
   a. production planning?
   b. production?
   c. inventory?
   d. purchasing?
4. Are there procedures for developing short- or medium-range manufacturing plans?
5. Does manufacturing management accept and understand these short- or medium-range plans?
6. Are manufacturing management efforts directed toward accomplishing these short- or medium-range plans?
7. Is performance against short- or medium-range plans measured periodically?
8. Are short- or medium-range manufacturing plans reviewed periodically to stay current?
9. Is the management by exception principle an integral part of short- or medium-range manufacturing plans?

C. Organization Structure:

1. Is the manufacturing organization chart compatible with other functional organization charts?
2. Is it clear who is charged with responsibility and who has authority over:
   a. production?
   b. production planning?
   c. inventory?
   d. purchasing?
3. Does each person in manufacturing know his or her job well?
4. Is it clear what the superior–subordinate relationships are in the manufacturing departments?
5. Are there adequate job descriptions for each manufacturing position?

YES   NO   N.A.

6. Is there a competent employee assigned to each manufacturing position? ___ ___ ___

7. Is the level of manufacturing training adequate for:
   a. management? ___ ___ ___
   b. employees? ___ ___ ___

8. Can the quality of manufacturing personnel be assessed for:
   a. management? ___ ___ ___
   b. employees? ___ ___ ___

9. Are the manufacturing departments adequately staffed? ___ ___ ___

10. Are reporting relationships clearly defined and understood by manufacturing personnel? ___ ___ ___

11. Is manufacturing management held accountable for its actions? ___ ___ ___

12. Is there provision within the manufacturing departments for periodic review of their organization structure? ___ ___ ___

D. Leadership:

1. Does manufacturing management provide the necessary leadership so that workers have a feeling of responsibility for accomplishing production goals? ___ ___ ___

2. Is effective leadership evident in these manufacturing areas:
   a. production? ___ ___ ___
   b. production planning? ___ ___ ___
   c. inventory? ___ ___ ___
   d. purchasing? ___ ___ ___

3. Does manufacturing management provide the necessary leadership so that company workers have favorable attitudes toward the organization and their fellow workers? ___ ___ ___

4. Does manufacturing management provide a feeling of freedom for workers to discuss job-related problems with their supervisors? ___ ___ ___

5. Does manufacturing management support its workers, that is, is there supportive behavior toward workers? ___ ___ ___

6. Does manufacturing management utilize some type of rewards and incentives to motivate workers? ___ ___ ___

                                                    YES   NO   N.A.

E. Communication:

1. Are manufacturing goals well com-
   municated to production personnel?   ___   ___   ___
2. Are fluctuations in current sales re-
   flected immediately in manufacturing
   operations in order to increase or decrease productive capacity?   ___   ___   ___
3. Are *downward* and *upward* channels of
   communication evident in:
   a. production?   ___   ___   ___
   b. production planning?   ___   ___   ___
   c. inventory?   ___   ___   ___
   d. purchasing?   ___   ___   ___
4. Have more efficient methods and pro-
   cesses of manufacture been communicated from engineering or purchasing personnel to production
   management?   ___   ___   ___
5. Has the company's program to obtain
   improvement, simplification, and economies in the following areas been well
   communicated to the appropriate personnel:
   a. materials?   ___   ___   ___
   b. labor?   ___   ___   ___
   c. overhead?   ___   ___   ___
6. Is an effective information system being
   used to relay important managerial production reports on a timely basis?   ___   ___   ___
7. Does the company employ some type of
   communications package program to
   keep employees informed and satisfied
   on the job?   ___   ___   ___

F. Control:

1. Is there adequate control over manufacturing goals so that they are in conformity with overall organization objec-
   tives?   ___   ___   ___
2. Are there effective control reports,
   methods, and techniques utilized for
   the following manufacturing areas:
   a. production?   ___   ___   ___
   b. production planning?   ___   ___   ___
   c. inventory?   ___   ___   ___
   d. purchasing?   ___   ___   ___
3. Is close control maintained over manufacturing costs?   ___   ___   ___

                                          YES   NO   N.A.

4. Are predetermined standards compared
   to actual results (budget versus actual)
   on a timely basis?   ___   ___   ___
5. Is corrective action undertaken when
   significant manufacturing deviations
   are detected?

II. PRODUCTION PLANNING   ___   ___   ___

   A. Long-Range Plans:

      1. Is production planning management of
         sufficient caliber to meet long-range
         manufacturing objectives?   ___   ___   ___
      2. Is there a continuous and sound program
         for production planning and schedul-
         ing?   ___   ___   ___
      3. Is production planning and scheduling
         an integral part of an information sys-
         tem?   ___   ___   ___
      4. Are production plans made as far in ad-
         vance as possible to:
         a. ensure availability of materials?   ___   ___   ___
         b. level machine loading?   ___   ___   ___
         c. minimize movement of workers?   ___   ___   ___
      5. Is there an effort to level out production
         over time?   ___   ___   ___
      6. Have there been adequate production
         planning and scheduling in the past to
         meet customer delivery dates?   ___   ___   ___

   B. Short- or Medium-Range Plans:

      1. Is there a centralized production plan-
         ning group whose focus is on current
         or short-range manufacturing opera-
         tions?   ___   ___   ___
      2. Is production planning management of
         sufficient caliber to meet short- or me-
         dium-range manufacturing objectives?   ___   ___   ___
      3. Do manufacturing plans provide for
         meeting scheduled completion dates?   ___   ___   ___
      4. Are current production plans made as
         far as possible in advance to:
         a. ensure availability of materials?   ___   ___   ___
         b. level loading of equipment?   ___   ___   ___
         c. minimize movement of workers?   ___   ___   ___
      5. Are mathematical techniques, such as
         MRP (materials requirements planning),
         linear programming, and simulation,
         employed to plan production efficiently
         and effectively?   ___   ___   ___

YES   NO   N.A.

6. Is there ample provision for locating customer orders during the manufacturing process? — — —

7. Are backlog figures charted as a guide for future production planning? — — —

8. Does the production planning group consider work in process so as to keep costs at a minimum? — — —

C. Organization Structure:

  1. Is the production planning department under the direction of a qualified manager? — — —

  2. Is the production planning department organized so that it can respond to changing conditions? — — —

  3. Is the production planning department organized so that production schedules are made as far as possible in advance to ensure efficient and economical manufacturing operations? — — —

  4. Are production schedules an integral part of an information system? — — —

  5. Are production schedules sufficiently comprehensive to include all customer orders (small to large size)? — — —

D. Leadership:

  1. Is the production planning manager a leader, i.e., does he or she exert the necessary leadership to accomplish established production quotas as well as deadlines? — — —

  2. Is leadership evident in the production planning function, that is, do production personnel look to this group as an effective source of information on production scheduling and control? — — —

  3. Is there appropriate interaction with a high degree of confidence and trust between the production planning group and production personnel? — — —

  4. Does the production planning group enlist the necessary cooperation of all manufacturing units to realize production goals? — — —

  5. Does the production planning group avoid wasted production time through effective planning and scheduling methods? — — —

6. Is the production planning group flexible enough to meet demands placed on it by the sales department? ___ ___ ___

E. Communication:

1. Are *downward* and *upward* communication channels used effectively to keep appropriate production personnel abreast of pertinent production schedules? ___ ___ ___
2. Does the production planning group communicate a sufficient flow of current manufacturing information to production personnel to achieve economy and efficiency in ongoing operations? ___ ___ ___
3. Are production schedules communicated far enough in advance to ensure:
   a. availability of materials? ___ ___ ___
   b. leveling of machine loading? ___ ___ ___
   c. keeping of overtime to a minimum? ___ ___ ___
4. Is production planning flexible enough to meet unanticipated changes that are transmitted periodically from different functional areas of the company? ___ ___ ___
5. Is feedback of deviations from production plans an essential part of the production planning process? ___ ___ ___

F. Control:

1. Is close control exercised by the production planning manager over production schedules? ___ ___ ___
2. Is there a periodic schedule for controlling manufacturing operations? ___ ___ ___
3. Is this periodic schedule:
   a. understood by operating personnel? ___ ___ ___
   b. followed by operating personnel? ___ ___ ___
4. Are production planning goals compared to actual production schedules so that corrective action can be undertaken if results are below expectations? ___ ___ ___
5. Are standard setup and run times used for loading the manufacturing (management control) centers? ___ ___ ___

YES   NO   N.A.

6. Does the machine loading system effectively balance the amount of machine capacity available?

7. Are delinquent production loads effectively rescheduled?

8. Are there enough production expediters to control ongoing manufacturing operations effectively?

9. Is there adequate control over production order backlogs?

10. Are the latest mathematical techniques, such as MRP (materials requirements planning) and simulation, employed to control ongoing manufacturing operations in an efficient and economical manner?

11. Are jobs scheduled by the production planning manager contained in the production schedules?

III. PRODUCTION

A. Long-Range Plans:

1. Are manufacturing facilities adequate to meet long-range company objectives?

2. Are manufacturing facilities well laid out to provide efficiency in:
   a. production?
   b. materials handling?
   c. related manufacturing functions?

3. Have production operations been free of bottlenecks?

4. Are manufacturing facilities capable of meeting long-range customer demands?

5. Are long-range manufacturing plans directed toward acquiring new:
   a. plant?
   b. equipment?
   c. tooling?

6. Does manufacturing management have a set procedure for replacing inefficient:
   a. plant?
   b. equipment?
   c. tooling?

7. Is factory automation utilized to the fullest extent?

YES   NO   N.A.

8. Are long-range manufacturing plans directed toward manufacturing facilities that are:
   a. well lighted?   ___ ___ ___
   b. well ventilated?   ___ ___ ___
   c. well maintained?   ___ ___ ___
9. Does production have a long-range preventive maintenance (PM) program?   ___ ___ ___
10. Can present capacity be expanded to meet long-range production needs?   ___ ___ ___
11. Do manufacturing facilities lend themselves to:
   a. a quality control program?   ___ ___ ___
   b. utilization of minicomputers to control automated machines and processes?   ___ ___ ___
   c. numerical control machine tools?   ___ ___ ___
12. Does production have capable managers as:
   a. plant superintendents?   ___ ___ ___
   b. work center supervisors?   ___ ___ ___
   c. foremen?   ___ ___ ___
13. Are manufacturing methods subject to constant scrutiny for improvement?   ___ ___ ___
14. Does the company employ an effective wage incentive system to keep costs at a minimum?   ___ ___ ___
15. Have the company's manufacturing facilities been operating at a desired level of capacity?   ___ ___ ___

B. Short- or Medium-Range Plans:
1. Do short- or medium-range manufacturing plans call for leveling out production?   ___ ___ ___
2. Do short- or medium-range manufacturing plans reduce or eliminate production bottlenecks?   ___ ___ ___
3. Do short- or medium-range manufacturing plans include a preventive maintenance (PM) program?   ___ ___ ___
4. Is there adequate provision for repairs and service of equipment that has high downtime?   ___ ___ ___
5. Is there ample provision for:
   a. expanding production?   ___ ___ ___
   b. contracting production?   ___ ___ ___
6. Is there an effective program to remedy:

	YES	NO	N.A.
a. high scrappage rate?	—	—	—
b. high rejection rate?	—	—	—
7. Is there a program to train employees who are not working efficiently?	—	—	—
8. Is there a program for promoting factory personnel?	—	—	—
9. Do short- or medium-range manufacturing plans provide a method for comparing actual times to standard times?	—	—	—
10. Are manufacturing methods subject to constant scrutiny for improvement?	—	—	—
11. Are manufacturing methods designed for economy of manufacture?	—	—	—
12. Do short- or medium-range manufacturing plans call for increasing worker productivity?	—	—	—
13. Do short- or medium-range manufacturing plans call for good health and safety practices in the manufacturing process?	—	—	—
14. Are current quality control techniques adequate?	—	—	—

C. Organization Structure:

	YES	NO	N.A.
1. Are production facilities well laid out to provide efficient and economical manufacturing?	—	—	—
2. Are production facilities organized so that materials handling is kept to a minimum?	—	—	—
3. Are production facilities organized so that there is an effective preventive maintenace (PM) program?	—	—	—
4. Are production facilities flexible enough to:			
a. accommodate shifts in product demand?	—	—	—
b. expand production?	—	—	—
c. contract production?	—	—	—
5. Is there a definite production program to obtain improvement, simplification, and economies in:			
a. equipment and machinery?	—	—	—
b. manufacturing processes?	—	—	—
c. raw materials?	—	—	—
d. direct and indirect labor?	—	—	—
e. manufacturing overhead?	—	—	—

YES   NO   N.A.

6. Do productive operations employ some type of wage-incentive system for manufacturing efficiency? ___ ___ ___

7. Are production facilities geared to utilize the latest technological developments, such as automatic machines, mechanical robots, and minicomputers? ___ ___ ___

8. Are production facilities well maintained so as to be safe and free from fire, explosion, and the like? ___ ___ ___

9. Is the plant well lighted and ventilated? ___ ___ ___

10. Is there security against strikes, sabotage, and the like? ___ ___ ___

D. Leadership:

1. Is there leadership evident in the production function, that is, do production personnel feel a real responsibility for production goals and behave in ways to implement them? ___ ___ ___

2. Do production personnel feel free to discuss their jobs and related problems with their supervisors? ___ ___ ___

3. Is there a friendly interaction between management and personnel with a degree of confidence and trust? ___ ___ ___

4. Is the appropriate style of leadership used for various types of production workers:
   a. autocratic (no participation in decisions)? ___ ___ ___
   b. consultative (some degree of participation in decisions)? ___ ___ ___
   c. participative (large degree of participation in decisions)? ___ ___ ___

5. Is there a high degree of teamwork, encouraged by effective leadership at the production level? ___ ___ ___

6. Do production supervisors give the necessary leadership to initiate improvements in work methods? ___ ___ ___

7. Do production supervisors give the necessary leadership to provide economy and efficiency of performance within the production work centers? ___ ___ ___

8. Do production supervisors back up their workers in conflict situations? ___ ___ ___

	YES	NO	N.A.

9. Do production supervisors maintain an open atmosphere to keep labor grievances and complaints to a minimum?

E. Communication:

1. Do production workers feel free to communicate their problems, whether they be job-related or personal, to their superiors?

2. Have the most efficient manufacturing methods and processes been communicated to production personnel?

3. Is the feedback concept utilized to hold production personnel accountable for their operations?

4. Have the detailed aspects of the incentive system been fully explained to production personnel?

5. Has a preventive maintenance program been communicated to all production personnel?

6. Have good safety practices been communicated to all production personnel for their protection?

7. Have good "housekeeping" procedures been communicated to all production personnel for increasing productivity?

F. Control:

1. Are production operations integrated with major input sources:
   a. engineering?
   b. inventory?
   c. purchasing?

2. Are actual manufacturing times compared to standard times as quickly as possible?

3. Is immediate corrective action undertaken once the deficiency is detected?

4. Do production reports, methods, and techniques lend themselves to economy and efficiency in ongoing manufacturing operations?

5. Is there adequate control over manufacturing operations to reduce or eliminate production bottlenecks?

6. Does effective control over production include a preventive maintenance (PM) program?

	YES	NO	N.A.

7. Are modern handling methods utilized for transportation of in-process manufactured items? ____ ____ ____

8. Is there effective control over the movement of in-process manufactured items? ____ ____ ____

9. Is the plant well laid out so as to permit materials flow in the most direct route from receiving through production to shipping? ____ ____ ____

10. Is the quality control mechanism adequate for producing products of uniform quality? ____ ____ ____

11. Are statistical quality control techniques used to monitor products at strategic control points? ____ ____ ____

12. Is there control over production rejects and rework? ____ ____ ____

13. Is there adequate review of product quality reports with the view of improving operational manufacturing performance? ____ ____ ____

IV. INVENTORY   ____ ____ ____

A. Long-Range Plans:

1. Is inventory management sufficiently qualified to meet long-range company objectives? ____ ____ ____

2. Are long-range inventory management plans coordinated with:
   a. production? ____ ____ ____
   b. purchasing? ____ ____ ____
   c. finance? ____ ____ ____

3. Is inventory properly and efficiently stored so as to provide a minimum of:
   a. obsolescence? ____ ____ ____
   b. deterioration? ____ ____ ____
   c. pilferage? ____ ____ ____

4. Is there an adequate inventory system under management control to plan inventory in the long run at optimum levels? ____ ____ ____

5. Is there an effective physical inventory system to obviate any surprises in loss or value? ____ ____ ____

6. Are inventory plans and procedures audited periodically by:
   a. internal auditors? ____ ____ ____
   b. external auditors? ____ ____ ____

	YES	NO	N.A.

B. Short- or Medium-Range Plans:

1. Is inventory management sufficiently qualified to meet short- or medium-range company objectives?
2. Are short-range inventory management plans an integral part of:
   a. production?
   b. purchasing?
3. Are inventories under control as to:
   a. type?
   b. amount?
4. Is there an adequate inventory system to:
   a. plan current inventory at optimum levels?
   b. compare physical to perpetual inventories?
   c. detect theft?
5. Are lead times figured into inventory levels for:
   a. purchasing?
   b. manufacturing?
6. Is the concept of safety stock employed as a protection against stockouts?
7. Are inventory levels coordinated with reorder points?
8. Are bills of materials utilized to determine inventory requirements?
9. Do short-range inventory plans include "make" versus "buy" decisions to lower costs?
10. Is receiving and inspection of inventory items adequate?

C. Organization Structure:

1. Is the inventory department under the direction of a capable manager?
2. Are inventories and their in-plant movements organized and reported by their basic types:
   a. raw materials?
   b. work in process?
   c. finished goods?
3. Are inventories maintained at their optimum level by their basic types:
   a. raw materials?
   b. work in process?
   c. finished goods?

YES   NO   N.A.

4. Is there an effective system of physical inventory to disclose any irregularities or losses? ____ ____ ____

5. Is inventory organized around the ABC method of classifying materials, i.e., by high-, medium-, and low-value items? ____ ____ ____

6. Is inventory integrated within an information system? ____ ____ ____

7. Are modern materials-handling methods used for transportation and storage of materials? ____ ____ ____

D. Leadership:

1. Does inventory management exert the necessary leadership to keep inventory under control? ____ ____ ____

2. Is inventory management capable of giving the leadership necessary to minimize the investment in:
   a. raw-materials inventories? ____ ____ ____
   b. work-in-process inventories? ____ ____ ____
   c. finished-goods inventories? ____ ____ ____

3. Is inventory kept at a minimum that is consistent with efficient production planning? ____ ____ ____

4. Does inventory management have the necessary clout to store inventories properly in order to minimize losses caused by spoilage, obsolescence, or depreciation? ____ ____ ____

5. Is inventory management sufficiently progressive to employ the most modern materials-handling methods for transportation and storage of inventories? ____ ____ ____

E. Communication:

1. Is there an information system utilized that employs efficient management methods and techniques to control inventories and to prepare periodic inventory reports that are of great value to management? ____ ____ ____

2. Is there an effective communication system designed to assist in keeping the inventory turnover rate high? ____ ____ ____

3. Is there good managerial control over movement of work-in-process materials so that this inventory is kept at a minimum? ____ ____ ____

YES   NO   N.A.

4. Is the level of work-in-process materials consistent with an efficient manufacturing cycle?   ____ ____ ____

5. Is there a procedure for highlighting excess inventory quantities and bringing this condition to management's attention in order to return them to their proper levels?   ____ ____ ____

6. Is there an effective inventory system for keeping any surprises in inventory losses to a minimum?   ____ ____ ____

F. Control:

1. Are inventory management control reports, methods, and techniques integrated with:
   a. production?   ____ ____ ____
   b. purchasing?   ____ ____ ____

2. Are inventories effectively controlled as to:
   a. type?   ____ ____ ____
   b. amount?   ____ ____ ____

3. Are inventories properly stored to provide a minimum of:
   a. obsolescence?   ____ ____ ____
   b. deterioration?   ____ ____ ____
   c. pilferage?   ____ ____ ____

4. Have inventory levels been reduced by profitable disposition of obsolete or excess items?   ____ ____ ____

5. Is inventory control integrated with:
   a. economic order quantities?   ____ ____ ____
   b. reorder points?   ____ ____ ____

6. Is the concept of safety stock employed to protect against stockouts?   ____ ____ ____

7. Are lead times figured into inventory levels?   ____ ____ ____

8. Have steps been taken to balance the cost generated by too small an inventory against the cost of carrying excessive inventories to determine an optimum inventory turnover?   ____ ____ ____

9. Are bills of materials utilized to determine what items should be retrieved from inventory?   ____ ____ ____

10. Is there adequate management control over the receipt of raw materials and parts from vendors?   ____ ____ ____

	YES	NO	N.A.

11. Is there adequate management control over the receipt of work-in-process items for the manufacturing departments?

12. Is there adequate inspection of items received into inventory as to:
    a. type?
    b. number?

13. Are inventory items physically counted to make sure that perpetual inventory records are accurate?

14. Is inventory controlled through the use of the ABC concept (A = high-value items, B = medium-value items, and C = low-value items)?

15. Is there an effective management control system for receiving materials that are not on a purchase order, i.e., products returned by customers?

16. Are materials available when needed for the start of production?

V. PURCHASING

A. Long-Range Plans:

1. Is purchasing management sufficiently qualified to meet long-range company objectives?

2. Are long-range purchasing plans coordinated with:
   a. production?
   b. inventory?
   c. finance?

3. Are managerial methods employed to keep routine purchasing tasks at a minimum?

4. Are appropriate management planning methods employed by purchasing?

5. Is there a purchasing performance program to measure the long-term performance of:
   a. vendors?
   b. buyers?
   c. purchased parts?

6. Do company buyers (over the long run) search for:

	YES	NO	N.A.

a. new sources of supply?

b. new and better materials and methods?

c. lower prices?

B. Short- or Medium-Range Plans:

1. Is purchasing management sufficiently qualified to meet short- or medium-range company objectives?

2. Are short- or medium-range purchasing plans an integral part of:
   a. production?
   b. inventory?
   c. finance?

3. Do purchasing models employ the economic order quantity (EOQ) concept?

4. Are bids obtained on large quantity purchases?

5. Do purchasing plans include provision for taking advantage of quantity discounts?

6. Does purchasing evaluate several sources of supply before issuing purchase orders?

7. Is there a set policy for ordering through purchasing requisitions?

C. Organization Structure:

1. Is the purchasing department under the direction of a capable manager?

2. Are purchasing procedures organized around searching for:
   a. new sources of supply?
   b. new materials?
   c. better manufacturing methods?
   d. lower prices (in the manufacturing process)?

3. Are purchasing procedures integrated within an information system?

4. Is the quality of goods considered when purchasing?

5. Are delivery times considered when purchasing?

6. Is there a managerial approach to measuring purchasing performance of buyers?

YES   NO   N.A.

7. Do purchasing procedures take into account automatic checks and balances
   (internal control) for matching orders
   and invoices?   ___   ___   ___

D. Leadership:
   1. Does purchasing management exert the
      necessary leadership to require that
      materials and supplies be in on time
      from suppliers?   ___   ___   ___
   2. Does the purchasing group provide the
      necessary leadership to take advantage
      of special buying opportunities that will
      lower overall product costs?   ___   ___   ___
   3. Does the purchasing group keep
      abreast of technological developments
      so as to alert the company's engineer-
      ing department to the existence of raw
      materials and processes?   ___   ___   ___
   4. Does the purchasing group search for
      newer and lower-cost sources of sup-
      ply?   ___   ___   ___
   5. Does the purchasing department em-
      ploy low-cost methods of preparing
      purchase orders?   ___   ___   ___

E. Communication:
   1. Is there an open atmosphere in which
      the purchasing group wants to keep
      abreast of technological developments
      and is constantly searching for:
      a. new sources of supply?   ___   ___   ___
      b. new and better materials?   ___   ___   ___
   2. Do purchasing agents spend ample
      time talking to salespersons in order to
      acquire sufficient information about
      new products and processes that may
      be beneficial to the company?   ___   ___   ___
   3. Do purchasing agents communicate in-
      formation about new products and pro-
      cesses to the proper authorities, such
      as inventory and engineering manage-
      ment, in order to keep manufacturing
      operations as efficient and economical
      as possible?   ___   ___   ___
   4. Are the results of purchasing perfor-
      mance communicated to the purchas-
      ing agents and their superiors?   ___   ___   ___

	YES	NO	N.A.

F. Control:

1. Are production control reports, methods, and techniques integrated with purchasing? ⎯ ⎯ ⎯

2. Is purchasing of large dollar amounts under the control of economic ordering formulas? ⎯ ⎯ ⎯

3. Does purchasing take advantage of quantity discounts? ⎯ ⎯ ⎯

4. Are there set managerial policies for buying from the outside? ⎯ ⎯ ⎯

5. Is purchasing performance by the company's purchasing agents under the control of a purchasing manager? ⎯ ⎯ ⎯

6. Is there adequate control exercised by purchasing management to ensure that:
   a. low prices are being paid for purchased items? ⎯ ⎯ ⎯
   b. new and better materials and parts are being bought? ⎯ ⎯ ⎯
   c. new sources of supply are being used? ⎯ ⎯ ⎯

7. Are there adequate controls, that is, checks and balances, for:
   a. issuing purchase orders? ⎯ ⎯ ⎯
   b. inspection of receipts? ⎯ ⎯ ⎯
   c. matching of orders, invoices, and receiving reports? ⎯ ⎯ ⎯

sections of the manufacturing management audit questionnaire are presented for the XYZ Company. In this chapter, applications center on short-range manufacturing plans and the organization of production.

COMMENTS ON THE MANUFACTURING QUESTIONNAIRE

Manufacturing Overview

In a manufacturing environment, purchased materials and manufactured materials for stock flow into the various stages of the production process. As they do, the materials take on a variety of forms and shapes until they become finished goods. Next, the finished products flow through the distribution system until they reach the customers. From this view, the focus is on the *materials* flow. Coupled with the materials flow is the corresponding *information* flow, a most important factor in coordinating the diversified manufacturing activities. Information must be comprehensive so as to allow integrated decision making throughout the entire materials-flow process. With this integrated flow of essential information, management and operating personnel can make adjustments swiftly and effectively in response to the ever-changing business environment.

This initial section of the manufacturing management audit questionnaire examines the major parts of the manufacturing function and its relation to other functional areas. The opening section is related not only to production planning and production, but also to inventory and purchasing. Similarly, it can be related to the sale and distribution of finished goods as set forth in Chapter 5. Also, it is intimately related to accounting (see Chapter 4). Overall, this beginning manufacturing overview section is an integral part of the materials- and information-flow evaluation.

Production Planning

The evaluation of the production planning group (see section II of the manufacturing management audit questionnaire in Figure 7-1) starts with examining the competency of its management. Important questions relating to long-range production plans are set forth for evaluation, followed by analogous questions on short- to medium-range plans. Ultimately, these short- to long-range planning questions evaluate the caliber of the production planning group and their ability to undertake their assigned tasks.

In the next subsection of the questionnaire, the production planning organization structure is reviewed. Is it flexible enough to meet changing conditions as well as ensure efficient and economical manufacturing operations? Building upon these subsections, the adequacy of leadership by the production planning group is assessed. Specifically, questions are asked to determine if production planning management provides the necessary leadership to achieve desired production goals. Complementary to the leadership subsection is the capacity of the group to communicate important information to manufacturing departments for economy and efficiency in ongoing operations.

The last subsection examines the degree of control over manufacturing operations. Not only is there a need for reviewing the adequacy of production planning schedules, but also there must be a means of determining if current schedules are below expectations so that corrective action can be taken.

Production

In the third section of the manufacturing management audit questionnaire, the production function is examined. Initially, it is evaluated in terms of its long-range plans. The focus is on the capability of manufacturing facilities to meet the long-term needs of the organization. Similarly, attention is paid to the human element with great emphasis on providing capable managers to control future ongoing operations. These same types of questions are asked on a short-term basis, namely, for short- to medium-range plans.

The main focus of the next subsection of the questionnaire is on the effectiveness of the organization structure for meeting production goals. For the most part, questions are asked that relate to the capabilities of the production facilities to provide efficient and economical manufacturing. Going beyond the organization structure, leadership, or lack thereof, in the production function is analyzed in the next subsection. Questions relating to the degree of teamwork between production management and its subordinates are asked. Overall, leadership of production supervisors focuses on the economy and efficiency of operations within the various production work centers.

For effective leadership, there is need for open channels of communication, the subject of the next subsection. The accent is on communicating efficient methods and processes, as well as on communicating worker-related problems to the proper management level for resolution. In the last subsection, the control factors over production are assessed. Specifically, questions relate to the comparing of actual manufacturing times to standard times, undertaking corrective action if deemed necessary, utilizing efficient production methods and techniques, employing quality control techniques at strategic control points, and so forth. Overall, the accent is on evaluating how well ongoing manufacturing operations are controlled as goods in process move from one work station to another.

Inventory

Evaluation of an organization's inventory system through the management audit questionnaire (see section IV of Figure 7-1) starts with determining the degree of integration of inventory management plans with other functional areas. Additional questions focus on such areas as the adequacy of inventory management to plan in the long run for optimum inventory levels. Translating the long-range inventory plans into a shorter time frame, typical questions are raised concerning the adequacy or short- to medium-range inventory plans to meet the requirements of purchasing and manufacturing as well as the need for protection against inventory stockouts. In addition, there are questions evaluating the compatibility of the inventory structure with short- to long-range plans.

Building upon the foregoing subsections of the questionnaire, the capability of inventory management to exert the necessary leadership to minimize the inventory investments is assessed. Complementary to this subsection is one on communication, whose purpose is to determine if proper information is forwarded to management for keeping inventory under control. In the final subsection, the degree of control over inventory is examined. If an out-of-control condition exists, appropriate management action can be undertaken so as to restore the inventory situation to normal.

Purchasing

The purchasing section concludes the manufacturing management audit questionnaire. An all-inclusive long-range purchasing plan should include close coordination with production, inventory, and finance. Questions relating to the utilization of managerial methods by purchasing are stressed for the long run. In turn, questions that assess the degree of the current year's (or intermediate years') purchasing plans are set forth. Next, questions that focus on the structure found in the purchasing department are used for evaluation. The main focus of this subsection relates to the competency of purchasing management to carry out its assigned activities.

In the next subsection, purchasing leadership is examined from many managerial viewpoints. Does purchasing management exercise sufficient control over its suppliers, and does it try to minimize costs of purchased materials and supplies? Even though purchasing management may be progressive in its approach to buying from the outside, there must be an open atmosphere for passing on important purchasing information to the appropriate managers and operating personnel. Questions relating to this area are covered in the subsection on communication. The final subsection on control evaluates purchasing control, whereby the accent is on keeping overall costs of purchased goods and services at a minimum.

Application of Management Audit Questionnaire to Short-Range Manufacturing Plans

As discussed in Chapter 5, the basic recommendation of implementing an improved long-range marketing plan was accepted by the chief executive officer of the XYZ Company. However, the president raised several questions about related plans, in particular those for the short run. Most importantly, is it possible to produce and distribute specialized products (private label) in the coming year? The president feels there is adequate manpower in research & development and engineering to handle the development of at least one or two new specialized products, but he is not too certain about production capabilities. Therefore, it may be necessary to go outside for initial production runs.

In view of this problem, the president again turned to the board consultant for an answer. As with previous problems, the consultant used a section of a management audit questionnaire, specifically, the short-range planning subsection on production (see Figure 7-2). Examination of the completed questionnaire section indicates that, on the surface, manufacturing operations are effective in producing finished goods, since most questions have been answered in the affirmative. However, closer scrutiny reveals a somewhat different situation.

Short-range manufacturing plans do not reduce or eliminate production bottlenecks (see question 2). Similarly, manufacturing facilities within the coming year are not capable of being expanded (see question 5). An interview with the manufacturing vice president revealed that all plants have inadequate manufacturing facilities for projected sales in the coming year. Because each plant has an attached warehouse, unused manufacturing areas over the past three years have been used as warehousing space. In fact, storage of finished goods is now at a critical stage. Any attempt to free these areas for manufacture of specialized products will necessitate renting substantial outside warehouse space at a premium. Overall, production bottlenecks have occurred, and manufacturing facilities are not capable of being expanded in the short run to produce the anticipated volume of specialized products.

Because of these factors, questions 10 through 12 show additional unfavorable responses. Manufacturing methods have not been subject to constant scrutiny for improvement, due to the fact that the engineering department lacked the time required for this task. Similarly, manufacturing methods are not currently designed for economy, partially because finished goods block the aisles of the work centers. At this point, finished goods are stacked in front of raw materials, and valuable production time is spent finding and retrieving the materials. The net result of these crowded conditions, especially before the shipping of seasonal merchandise, is a decrease in worker productivity.

Recommendations to Improve Short-Range Manufacturing Plans

In light of these conditions, the consultant's initial recommendation to utilize present manufacturing facilities for producing specialized products (private label) is certainly not feasible. In fact, the board consultant has uncovered some serious production problems that must be solved before consideration can be given to manufacturing these products. He is now

Figure 7-2. XYZ Company evaluation of production capabilities for specialized products.

	YES	NO	N.A.
PRODUCTION			

B. Short-Range Plans:

	YES	NO	N.A.
1. Do short-range manufacturing plans call for leveling out production?	X		
2. Do short-range manufacturing plans reduce or eliminate production bottlenecks?		X	
3. Do short-range manufacturing plans include a preventive maintenance (PM) program?	X		
4. Is there adequate provision for repairs and service of equipment?	X		
5. Is there ample provision for:			
a. expanding production?		X	
b. contracting production?	X		
6. Is there an effective program to remedy:			
a. high scrappage rate?	X		
b. high rejection rate?	X		
7. Is there a program to train employees who are not working efficiently?	X		
8. Is there a program for promoting factory personnel?	X		
9. Do short-range manufacturing plans provide a method for comparing actual times to standard times?	X		
10. Are manufacturing methods subject to constant scrutiny for improvement?		X	
11. Are manufacturing methods designed for economy of manufacture?		X	
12. Do short-range manufacturing plans call for increasing worker productivity?		X	
13. Do short-range manufacturing plans call for good health and safety practices in the manufacturing process?	X		
14. Are current quality control techniques adequate?	X		

Questionnaire Comments (Negative Answers):

Question 2   Unfortunately, short-range manufacturing plans do not include a provision for eliminating production bottlenecks which now exist in the plant. This condition has been caused in part by the need to store an increasing level of finished goods.

Question 5   Because of the need to store finished goods in the unused manufacturing areas, there are no immediate plans to free these areas for manufacturing new products. Outside storage space is available only at a premium.

Question 10   The engineering department lacks the time to scrutinize manufacturing methods for possible improvement.
Question 11   Because there is no planned approach to allocating plant space to manufacture and storage, plant operations have become somewhat less than economical.
Question 12   The engineering department lacks the time to investigate the efficiency of worker productivity.

---

recommending that the XYZ Company not only subcontract the specialized products for the coming year, but also review its production facilities so that present and future products can be produced efficiently and economically.

In retrospect, what originally appeared to be a simple and isolated marketing problem turned out to be a complex problem that interfaced with many of the company's functions, in particular, research & development, engineering, and manufacturing. Although not discussed in the foregoing analysis, all these areas are related to finance, especially flexible budgets for the coming year. Thus, the board consultant who was asked to solve a specific manufacturing problem has found that he has a "tiger by the tail." To assure best overall performance in such a situation, it is recommended that the problem under study be initially expanded so that the functional areas can be interrelated. This approach avoids the problem of optimizing one function (department) at the expense of suboptimizing for the entire company.

APPLICATION OF MANAGEMENT AUDIT QUESTIONNAIRE TO THE ORGANIZATION OF PRODUCTION

Last week, the XYZ Company's vice president in charge of production visited one of its major manufacturing facilities. The reason for his visit was the plant's manufacturing costs, which have risen much faster than for the other plants. This facility is producing four new products which, as of this date, have not been manufactured by the other plants. The vice president is trying to determine the cause of the plant's high manufacturing costs before permitting the other plants to start production on these new products. After a stormy session with the plant superintendent, the vice president felt that the real cause of the higher costs was not determined.

In view of these difficulties, the vice president sent his staff consultant to investigate the matter further and to recommend appropriate action to remedy high manufacturing costs. The staff member has decided to use a portion of the manufacturing management audit questionnaire, namely, the organization structure subsection on production. Inspection of the completed questions (see Figure 7-3) shows several negative answers that need to be analyzed further.

Both questions 1 and 2 were answered in the negative. The introduction of four new products has led to production line problems. The production line was set up years ago to handle the products at that time and has not been changed to accommodate the new products. Hence, once the new products go through the regular manufacturing operations, they must be moved to another department for adding the accessories not found on standard products. After completion, these new products must be moved again to the packaging area—another movement not found with the standard products. Also, the staff consultant found that the addition of accessories is causing problems in the packaging department, since the shipping containers were not meant to handle somewhat larger products. As a result, more time is spent on packaging the new products than on the present ones.

As the negative answers to parts of question 5 indicate, this manufacturing facility does not have a production program to obtain improvement, simplification, and economies in its manufacturing processes. Nor does it have such a program for direct and indirect labor and for manufacturing overhead. Failure to have such programs is responsible for the current difficulties.

The remaining questions were answered in the affirmative. Although not shown in this case study, the remaining subsections of the manufacturing management audit questionnaire were employed to ensure that all major problems had been identified before making final recommendations.

Recommendations to Improve the Organization of Production

Uncovering the major manufacturing difficulties took the staff consultant only two days. However, final recommendations to the vice president in charge of manufacturing were more difficult to develop. After extensive discussions with the manufacturing superintendent and his foremen, it was finally unanimously agreed that conveyor belts could be built to transport the semifinished products to the accessory department for final assembly before forwarding them to the packaging department. Hence, use of conveyor belts to save handling costs was the first recommendation. The consultant next recommended that a new type of package be designed to meet the requirements of the company's new products. Even though the cost of the new packaging will be slightly higher than the old, the reduction in labor costs will offset this cost by a considerable margin. Other recommendations based on other parts of the management audit questionnaire are in order, but the major deficiencies of this plant's operations have been resolved.

**Figure 7-3. XYZ Company evaluation of structure
of manufacturing facilities.**

	YES	NO	N.A.

PRODUCTION

C. Organization Structure:

	YES	NO	N.A.
1. Are production facilities well laid out to provide efficient and economical manufacturing?		X	
2. Are production facilities organized so that materials handling is kept to a minimum?		X	
3. Are production facilities organized so that there is an effective preventive maintenance (PM) program?	X		
4. Are production facilities flexible enough to:			
a. accommodate shifts in product demand?	X		
b. expand production?	X		
c. contract production?	X		
5. Is there a definite production program to obtain improvement, simplification, and economies in:			
a. equipment and machinery?	X		
b. manufacturing processes?		X	
c. raw materials?	X		
d. direct and indirect labor?		X	
e. manufacturing overhead?		X	
6. Do productive operations employ some type of wage incentive system for manufacturing efficiency?	X		
7. Are production facilities geared to utilize the latest technological developments, such as automatic machines, mechanical robots, and minicomputers?	X		
8. Are production facilities well maintained so as to be safe and free from fire, explosion, and the like?	X		
9. Is the plant well lighted and ventilated?	X		
10. Is there security against strikes, sabotage, and the like?	X		

Questionnaire Comments (Negative Answers):

Question 1   The four new products must be moved from the assembly department to another department for adding the accessories not found on the other products. After completion, they must be moved again to the packaging area.

Question 2   As indicated above, there is a dual physical movement of the

four new products that is not found with the regularly produced products. Also, there are problems in the packaging
department with the somewhat larger products.

Question 5   Since the company does not have a program to improve and
simplify manufacturing processes, it is incurring consider-
ably higher costs for its four new products.

SUMMARY

Although the main focus of this chapter has been on the presentation of the
manufacturing management audit questionnaire, it should be noted that
many other sections of the questionnaire are related directly or indirectly to
it. These include the sections found in the preceding and succeeding
chapters of the text. Those sections that relate directly to manufacturing are:
I. Manufacturing Overview, II. Production Planning, III. Production, IV.
Inventory, and V. Purchasing.

This division of manufacturing activities on the basis of the manufacturing management audit questionnaire with its many questions gives one the
capability of determining how well the major manufacturing areas are functioning, that is, whether they are meeting predetermined organization objectives.

As in previous chapters, selected sections of the questionnaire have been
applied to the XYZ Company, specifically, to short-range manufacturing
plans and the organization of production. As usual, the questionnaire is an
initiating point for making recommendations to overcome managerial and
operational deficiencies.

8

Evaluating the Personnel Function

EVALUATING THE PERSONNEL FUNCTION by utilizing a management audit questionnaire can be a difficult task, because the "people factor" can rarely be assessed completely. For one thing, the needs of the individuals who comprise the company's work force change continuously. Additionally, it should be noted that the personnel function does not operate alone, but rather is a most important part of each functional area.

For an objective evaluation of the personnel function in a typical organization, the following sections are presented in this chapter:

I. Personnel Overview
II. Manpower Planning
III. Industrial Relations

As with previous parts of the management audit questionnaire, they are developed from a broad perspective, thereby allowing the questionnaire, shown in Figure 8-1, to be usable for most situations.

Also, two sample applications of the personnel management audit questionnaire are again illustrated for the XYZ Company. Specifically, these include personnel leadership and marketing personnel communication. Appropriate recommendations are set forth to remedy the deficiencies detected.

COMMENTS ON THE PERSONNEL QUESTIONNAIRE

Personnel Overview

The personnel area has the capability to make or break any company. To succeed, the company requires a productive group of people who are highly

(text continues on page 179)

Figure 8-1. Management Audit Questionnaire: Personnel.

	YES	NO	N.A.

I. PERSONNEL OVERVIEW

  A. Long-Range Plans:

    1. Are long-range personnel plans in agreement with:
      a. long-range organization objectives? ___ ___ ___
      b. long-range plans of other functional areas? ___ ___ ___
      c. medium-range personnel plans? ___ ___ ___
      d. short-range personnel plans? ___ ___ ___
    2. Are long-range personnel plans reviewed by:
      a. board of directors? ___ ___ ___
      b. top management? ___ ___ ___
    3. Is there an official planning committee to develop long-range personnel plans? ___ ___ ___
    4. Does personnel management accept and understand these long-range plans? ___ ___ ___
    5. Are personnel management efforts directed toward accomplishing these long-range plans? ___ ___ ___
    6. Is performance against long-range personnel plans measured periodically? ___ ___ ___
    7. Are long-range personnel plans reviewed periodically so as to stay current? ___ ___ ___
    8. Is the management by exception principle an integral part of long-range personnel plans? ___ ___ ___

  B. Short- or Medium-Range Plans:

    1. Are short- or medium-range personnel plans in agreement with:
      a. short- or medium-range organization objectives? ___ ___ ___
      b. short- or medium-range plans of other functional areas? ___ ___ ___
      c. long-range personnel plans? ___ ___ ___
    2. Are short- or medium-range personnel plans reviewed by:
      a. top management? ___ ___ ___
      b. middle management? ___ ___ ___
      c. lower management? ___ ___ ___

	YES	NO	N.A.

3. Are there procedures for developing short- or medium-range personnel plans? ___ ___ ___

4. Does personnel management accept and understand these short- or medium-range plans? ___ ___ ___

5. Are personnel management efforts directed toward accomplishing these short- or medium-range plans? ___ ___ ___

6. Is performance against short- or medium-range plans measured periodically? ___ ___ ___

7. Are short- or medium-range personnel plans reviewed periodically to stay current? ___ ___ ___

8. Is the management by exception principle an integral part of short- or medium-range personnel plans? ___ ___ ___

C. Organization Structure:

1. Is the personnel organization chart compatible with other functional organization charts? ___ ___ ___

2. Is it clear who is charged with responsibility and who has authority over:
   a. personnel? ___ ___ ___
   b. manpower planning? ___ ___ ___
   c. industrial relations? ___ ___ ___

3. Does each person in personnel know his or her job well? ___ ___ ___

4. Is it clear what the superior–subordinate relationships are in the personnel department? ___ ___ ___

5. Are there adequate job descriptions for each personnel position? ___ ___ ___

6. Is there a competent employee assigned to each personnel position? ___ ___ ___

7. Is the level of personnel training adequate for:
   a. management? ___ ___ ___
   b. employees? ___ ___ ___

8. Can the quality of company personnel be assessed for:
   a. management? ___ ___ ___
   b. employees? ___ ___ ___

9. Is the personnel department adequately staffed? ___ ___ ___

YES   NO   N.A.

10. Are reporting relationships clearly defined and understood by personnel?   ____   ____   ____
11. Is personnel management held ac-
countable for its actions?   ____   ____   ____
12. Is there provision within the personnel
department for periodic review of its
organization structure?   ____   ____   ____

D. Leadership:

1. Does personnel management provide
the necessary leadership to have a formal program of personnel selection and
evaluation   before   hiring   new   em-
ployeees?   ____   ____   ____
2. Does personnel management give the
leadership necessary to have an annual
review of present personnel for the purpose of:
a. improving their performance?   ____   ____   ____
b. determining their promotions?   ____   ____   ____
c. determining their remunerations?   ____   ____   ____
3. Is personnel management sufficiently
progressive to have an ongoing training
program for developing:
a. management personnel?   ____   ____   ____
b. nonmanagement personnel?   ____   ____   ____
4. Does management exert its influence in
seeing that company personnel are ef-
fectively employed in their jobs?   ____   ____   ____
5. Does management exert its influence to
have an effective program that en-
lightens employees on the economic
"facts of life," i.e., relationship of their
pay to the cost-of-living index and the
impact of cost increases on the company's operations?   ____   ____   ____

E. Communication:

1. Do the downward channels of communication facilitate the accomplishment of company objectives and activities in an efficient and economical
manner?   ____   ____   ____
2. Do the upward channels of communication facilitate the accomplishment of company objectives and activities in an efficient and economical
manner?   ____   ____   ____

	YES	NO	N.A.

3. Are there downward and upward channels of communication to provide for an efficient flow of information on:
   a. company programs and projects? ____ ____ ____
   b. company policies and directives? ____ ____ ____
   c. work methods and procedures? ____ ____ ____
   d. matters affecting employee morale? ____ ____ ____
   e. matters affecting employee needs? ____ ____ ____
4. Are the general methods of communication effectively utilized:
   a. spoken or written words? ____ ____ ____
   b. numbers, including mathematics? ____ ____ ____
   c. pictures? ____ ____ ____
   d. actions? ____ ____ ____
5. Are there organization policies to encourage employees to express their views and recommendations through formal communication channels? ____ ____ ____
6. Are informal communication channels, i.e., the "grapevine," used to supplement the formal communication channels? ____ ____ ____
7. Do communication channels provide the necessary information that motivates employees to take *pride* in their work? ____ ____ ____
8. Do communication channels provide the necessary information that affects the employees' well-being, i.e., opportunity for advancement and seniority in a union? ____ ____ ____

F. Control:
   1. Is there adequate control exercised over personnel so that their objectives are in conformity with overall organization objectives? ____ ____ ____
   2. Are employees who are positively motivated given adequate control over their work environment to realize more of their needs on the job? ____ ____ ____
   3. Are effective control methods and techniques used in:
      a. personnel? ____ ____ ____
      b. manpower planning? ____ ____ ____
      c. industrial relations? ____ ____ ____
   4. Is close control maintained over personnel costs? ____ ____ ____

	YES	NO	N.A.

5. Are predetermined personnel standards compared to actual results (budget versus actual) on a timely basis? ____ ____ ____

6. Is corrective action undertaken when significant deviations are detected? ____ ____ ____

II. MANPOWER PLANNING ____ ____ ____

A. Long-Range Plans:

1. Is manpower planning management sufficiently qualified to meet long-range objectives? ____ ____ ____

2. Are manpower needs an integral part of the company's long-range plans? ____ ____ ____

3. Are manpower planning methods used to predict future personnel needs? ____ ____ ____

4. Are key positions protected with trained replacements? ____ ____ ____

5. Is there an effective training program for key (executive) personnel? ____ ____ ____

6. Is the company training program geared to handle future expansion? ____ ____ ____

B. Short- or Medium-Range Plans:

1. Is manpower planning management sufficiently qualified to meet short- or medium-range objectives? ____ ____ ____

2. Do short- or medium-range plans include a program for evaluating manpower requirements for the coming year? ____ ____ ____

3. Are there procedures for recruitment or selection of personnel to fill vacancies or new positions? ____ ____ ____

4. Do personnel plans include a provision for labor turnover? ____ ____ ____

5. Do personnel plans include a review of current wages to ensure compatibility with other companies in the area? ____ ____ ____

6. Do personnel plans regulate employee overtime so that it does not become excessive? ____ ____ ____

7. Is there an effective training program for plant personnel? ____ ____ ____

C. Organization Structure:

1. Is the manpower planning group under the direction of a capable manager? ____ ____ ____

2. Is manpower planning integrated with the corporate planning function? ____ ____ ____

	YES	NO	N.A.

3. Does the organization structure lend itself to on-the-job training to satisfy immediate and future job openings? — — —

4. Are personnel replacements being trained for continuity of operations? — — —

5. Does the company enjoy stable employment levels that minimize the problem of manpower replacement? — — —

6. Is manpower turnover acceptable to the company's management? — — —

D. Leadership:

1. Does personnel management feel a real responsibility for company goals and react in a way to implement them through effective manpower planning? — — —

2. Does personnel management exert the necessary influence to protect all key positions with trained replacements? — — —

3. Does the personnel department maintain an effective training program for all key personnel? — — —

4. Is the personnel department training new personnel for the expansion of its operations? — — —

5. Does the personnel department exert the required influence to see that first-line supervisors are:
   a. functioning effectively? — — —
   b. paid adequately? — — —

6. Is personnel management progressive enough to make sure that wage and salary rates plus fringe benefits compare favorably with:
   a. the area in which the company is located? — — —
   b. its competitors? — — —

7. Does personnel demand of top management fringe benefits that will attract top-notch employees? — — —

8. Does personnel management know and understand the problems of company employees well enough to realize their future impact on manpower planning? — — —

E. Communication:

1. Are recommendations for advancement communicated to the appropriate personnel? — — —

	YES	NO	N.A.

2. Does the company actively communicate new job openings internally before going to the outside? ___ ___ ___

3. Does the company state in its job openings the opportunities for learning new skills through company-sponsored training programs? ___ ___ ___

4. Does the company have a policy of publicizing promotions:
   a. within the company? ___ ___ ___
   b. outside the company? ___ ___ ___

F. Control:

1. Is there adequate control over manpower planning so that ample personnel are available to handle the current work load? ___ ___ ___

2. Is there adequate control over the recruitment and selection of personnel to fill vacancies or new positions? ___ ___ ___

3. Is an effort made to keep labor turnover to a minimum? ___ ___ ___

4. Is there effective control of employee overtime? ___ ___ ___

5. Is there effective managerial control over company training programs? ___ ___ ___

6. Are manpower plans related to actual results where possible so that corrective action can be undertaken if results are below expectations? ___ ___ ___

III. INDUSTRIAL RELATIONS ___ ___ ___

A. Long-Range Plans:

1. Is personnel management of a sufficient caliber to meet long-range industrial relations objectives? ___ ___ ___

2. Do personnel long-range plans include provision for improving relations with employees? ___ ___ ___

3. Does the company have a long-term program for providing adequate:
   a. training? ___ ___ ___
   b. medical care? ___ ___ ___
   c. vacations? ___ ___ ___
   d. insurance? ___ ___ ___
   e. pensions? ___ ___ ___
   f. sick pay? ___ ___ ___

	YES	NO	N.A.

4. Does the company continue to compete favorably with other firms in the area in terms of:
   a. wage rates?
   b. fringe benefits?
   c. layoff benefits?
5. Has the company had good relationships with its union(s)?

B. Short- or Medium-Range Plans:

   1. Is personnel management of a sufficient caliber to meet short- or medium-range industrial relations objectives?
   2. When employee relations are marginal or bad, do personnel plans call for improving them?
   3. Do plans call for an employee review program?
   4. Is there an annual job evaluation and review program?
   5. Do plans call for improving working conditions?
   6. Do plans call for improving employee fringe benefits?
   7. Do plans call for an effective health and safety program?
   8. Do plans include a program for improving employee morale and attitude toward the company if needed?
   9. Do plans call for formal procedures to resolve union–management conflicts about:
      a. wages?
      b. overtime?
      c. production rates?
      d. work rules?

C. Organization Structure:

   1. Is the industrial relations department under the direction of a capable manager?
   2. Does the company enjoy favorable relations with its:
      a. unionized employees?
      b. nonunionized employees?
   3. Does the company's wage and salary structure compare favorably with other firms?

YES   NO   N.A.

4. Does the company's fringe benefits structure compare favorably with other firms?   ___   ___   ___

5. Does the company's incentive system encourage:
   a. high productivity?   ___   ___   ___
   b. greater efficiency and economy of operation?   ___   ___   ___

6. Are employee handbooks used to reduce possible management–employee conflicts by having policies set forth in writing?   ___   ___   ___

D. Leadership:

1. Does top management exert its influence in maintaining good industrial relations with its employees?   ___   ___   ___

2. Is top management's interest in good industrial relations reflected in its:
   a. wage and salary structure?   ___   ___   ___
   b. fringe benefits?   ___   ___   ___

3. Is there harmony and cooperation evident in the company among its:
   a. employees?   ___   ___   ___
   b. departments?   ___   ___   ___

4. Are good industrial relations evidenced by high morale and positive attitudes of employees toward the firm?   ___   ___   ___

5. Do subordinates feel free to discuss important matters concerning themselves with their superiors?   ___   ___   ___

E. Communication:

1. Does the company actively promote a good relationship with its union(s)?   ___   ___   ___

2. Does the company actively promote harmony and cooperation among its employees and departments through appropriate communication channels?   ___   ___   ___

3. Do company employees feel free to communicate their personal and job-related problems to their superiors?   ___   ___   ___

4. Does the company promote on-the-job and off-the-job training as a part of its overall educational program?   ___   ___   ___

5. Does the company participate actively in worthy community projects?   ___   ___   ___

	YES	NO	N.A.

F. Control:

1. Does management exercise sufficient control over its industrial relations program so that it has a good relationship with its employees?

2. Is there an industrial relations program to maintain or improve the company's image in the eyes of its employees?

3. Does management exercise sufficient control over:
   a. employee wages?
   b. employee fringe benefits?
   c. employee working conditions?

4. Does management promote harmony and cooperation among its employees?

5. Are industrial relations programs related to actual results where possible so that corrective action can be undertaken if results are below expectations?

---

motivated to accomplish organization objectives. Similarly, it needs a work force that is capable of handling current and future work volumes. Implied in this is the need for flexibility: a permanent work force must be maintained for normal operations and supplemented with an auxiliary force when there are peak work loads or emergency conditions to be met. In this manner, management can keep personnel costs at a minimum while servicing the required business functions and subfunctions necessary to accomplish predetermined objectives.

The main purpose of this first section of the personnel management audit questionnaire is to focus on the capabilities of management to meet changing personnel conditions. The manner in which managers respond to these change factors is one way to evaluate their capabilities in handling organization personnel. In a few words, this beginning section evaluates not only how well the personnel function itself is operating, but also how effectively it is operating in the various functional areas of an organization.

Manpower Planning

To evaluate the manpower planning function through the management audit questionnaire (see section II of Figure 8-1) it is necessary to start assessing the capabilities of personnel management. Key questions relating to long-range manpower plans are set forth, followed by those relating to a shorter time frame—short- to medium-range. Fundamentally, these questions examine the adequacy of plans to meet manpower needs from the short run to long run. Building upon this background, the manpower planning structure is examined. Such questions as whether the organization structure lends itself to on-the-job training and whether personnel replacements are trained for continuity of operations are asked.

In the next subsection, questions relating to leadership by personnel management, in such areas as training programs and wage and salary rates, are developed. The emphasis here is on the quality of personnel management to achieve specific manpower plans. Supplementary to the leadership subsection is an evaluation of the company's communication process with its personnel. In the final subsection, the degree of control over manpower planning is reviewed. In effect, the main concern of these questions is to determine if qualified personnel, including managers, are available to keep the organization operating in an efficient and economical manner to meet predetermined objectives. If actual results are different from manpower plans, corrective action needs to be undertaken.

Industrial Relations

The industrial relations (IR) section of the personnel management audit questionnaire (see section III of Figure 8-1) is to a large degree an extension of the prior two sections. An all-inclusive personnel program should include a provision for maintaining as well as improving industrial relations. Questions relating to short-range and long-range industrial relations plans are initially asked. They center on determining if the company provides adequate employee and fringe benefits that compete favorably with firms in the same area and if there is a sufficient degree of harmony between management and its subordinates. Where the company does not meet established wages, benefits, and the like, questions are asked regarding the plans to improve them. Next, questions are asked regarding the wage and salary structure as related to encouraging high productivity as well as efficiency and economy of operation. Also, the relationship of this structure to other firms of comparable size is examined.

In the next subsection, industrial relations leadership is evaluated from several points of view. Is there harmony and cooperation in the company from effective IR management? Is top management interested in good industrial relations? And are good industrial relations evidenced by high morale and positive attitudes of employees? The next subsection examines the degree to which employees feel free to communicate their personnel and job-related problems to their supervisors. Within the last subsection, control over industrial relations programs is evaluated, that is, does management exert sufficient control over employee wages, benefits, and working conditions to promote harmony and cooperation among its employees and, ultimately, to meet organization objectives?

APPLICATION OF MANAGEMENT AUDIT QUESTIONNAIRE TO PERSONNEL LEADERSHIP

Just recently, Mr. Amsden took over as the vice president of personnel. He succeeds Mr. Winston, one of the founders of the XYZ Company. Early in his career, Mr. Winston hired Ms. Bertha Elsmere, a promising young employee, as his secretary. As Mr. Winston's career blossomed, so did his secretary's. She advanced with Winston, both in salary and responsibility. As Winston progressed, he relied more and more upon Ms. Elsmere. She became, in effect, his indispensable right hand.

Upon Winston's retirement, Amsden inherited Ms. Elsmere. He found her to be competent; in fact, she was so competent that she initiated personnel programs, answered his correspondence, and made appointments in Amsden's name in much the same manner as she had for Mr. Winston. Mr. Amsden soon realized that the more freedom and initiative Bertha was allowed to exercise, the more smoothly the office seemed to operate.

Ms. Elsmere's whole life had been dedicated to her career. Although she went to work immediately after graduation from high school, she had managed to accumulate both bachelor's and master's degrees in personnel. Before coming to the XYZ Company, she had worked for a large metropolitan insurance company. There, she quickly demonstrated ambition and technical competence. She also had proven a certain leadership capability in that she was elected business agent and finally president of the office workers union. Although the company is not unionized, she continued to retain close ties with the officials of the union. In a sense, this was her social life. She had never actively promoted the union at the XYZ Company, yet when the subject arose, she had been known to defend unionism vigorously as the only *real* voice in promoting the worker's welfare.

One reason why she had not actively promoted the union at the company was the special treatment that Mr. Winston had given her. She was the only person of secretarial status to have her own parking place, and she was also allowed to leave work twenty minutes early to beat the traffic across town. In addition, she seemed to make a deliberate effort to be the last of the secretaries to return from lunch and office breaks.

The central office staff consists of 26 women and 6 men. This group is known to be a bit casual with respect to work rules. In the past, this was overlooked because, as one vice president said, "they get their work done."

Lately, it has appeared that starting times are ignored more often than in the past, and casual conversation seems to be the main activity rather than a diversion. To make matters worse, the work is beginning to fall behind schedule.

In view of the foregoing facts, Mr. Amsden has been directed by the president to do something about the deteriorating office situation. In effect, the president's mandate is to shape up the clerical staff. Having at his disposal the personnel part of the management audit questionnaire, Mr. Amsden answered all three sections. However, he found that the leadership subsection of the personnel overview (see Figure 8-2) best highlights the foregoing difficulties.

The first question has been answered in the affirmative, since the company does have a formal program of personnel selection and evaluation before hiring new employees. In contrast, question 2, which pertains to management's insistence on annual reviews for improving employee performance, has been answered with no. Failure of the company to undertake an annual review of present corporate personnel is one of the causes of the deteriorating conditions. Although there is an ongoing program for promoting management and non-management personnel (see question 3), the company fails to make sure that employees are fully productive (question 4). Additionally, as noted in question 5, the basic educational process that relates corporate values received to salaries paid is lacking at corporate headquarters. Overall, this subsection of the questionnaire has been vital in helping Mr. Amsden to "get a handle" on the important problems confronting him about the corporate staff.

Recommendations to Improve Personnel Leadership

On the basis of the foregoing analysis, Mr. Amsden must consider recommendations not only for the entire clerical staff, but also for his secretary Ms. Elsmere. In essence, he must focus on an appropriate leadership style that can be applied to all company personnel. Perhaps, in terms of the functioning of the corporate office, the "unbounded" behavioral approach which allows Ms. Elsmere the autonomy to pursue her job is the most effective way to operate. The problem facing Mr. Amsden is, of course, how can he insist upon rigorous compliance with personnel policies when his own secretary fails to practice them? Should he not only insist that Ms. Elsmere comply, but also rescind her parking privilege? What will be her reaction? Needless to say, there is much in this case that will lead to a deeper understanding of the "price of leadership."

Although several approaches can be recommended for a solution, Mr. Amsden took the position that much of his secretary's behavior may be at-

Figure 8-2. XYZ Company evaluation of personnel leadership.

	YES	NO	N.A.

I. PERSONNEL OVERVIEW

    D. Leadership:

        1. Does personnel management provide the necessary leadership to have a formal program of personnel selection and evaluation before hiring new employees?   X

        2. Does personnel management give the leadership necessary to have an annual review of present personnel for the purpose of:

            a. improving their performance?   X

            b. determining their promotions?   X

            c. determining their remunerations?   X

        3. Is personnel management sufficiently progressive to have an ongoing program for developing:

            a. management personnel?   X

            b. nonmanagement personnel?   X

        4. Does management exert its influence in seeing that company personnel are effectively employed in their jobs?   X

        5. Does management exert its influence to have an effective program that enlightens employees on the economic "facts of life," i.e., relationship of their pay to the cost-of-living index and the impact of cost increases on the company's operations?   X

Questionnaire Comments (Negative Answers):

Question 2 (a)   Failure of the company to have an annual review of present corporate personnel that is directed at improving their performance is one of the causes for the deteriorating conditions at corporate headquarters.

Question 4   Even though management does an effective job of hiring personnel for specific positions, it fails to make sure that they are productive employees once they are hired. This condition appears to be extremely true of the corporate-level clerical staff.

Question 5   Although the traditional personnel functions are carried out, the basic educational process that relates corporate values received to salaries paid is lacking at headquarters.

tributable to an attempt on her part to demonstrate how important she is. It must be remembered that her former boss—a founder of the company—was gone. Anyone who has ever changed bosses knows that there is a period in which the individual strives to re-establish his or her credentials with the new incumbent. Mr. Amsden reasoned that if Bertha had an opportunity to demonstrate her capabilities, she would have no need to differentiate herself with special privileges. He therefore decided to give her a series of challenging assignments (in addition to her other work) to be completed in a rather short time, allow her to keep her parking spot, give her the choice of either quitting on time or starting one-half hour earlier in order to leave one-half hour earlier, and insist that breaks be only the alloted time. Initially Bertha grumbled a bit, but within a week, she was conforming.

During the following week, Mr. Amsden approached the office manager about the clerical staff problem. The recommendation could best be called "orientation," despite the fact that many of the staff had been there for a while. The program went back to basics—starting times, quitting times, personnel policies, benefits, and the like. The program was followed by one-on-one conferences between the manager and each member of the clerical staff. During these conferences specific goals were spelled out. Also, a performance evaluation program was instituted. (The final result was that over a six-month period, three girls quit and were never replaced. The rest of the staff seemed to absorb the work without real difficulty.)

APPLICATION OF MANAGEMENT AUDIT QUESTIONNAIRE TO MARKETING PERSONNEL COMMUNICATIONS

Just last week, the vice president in charge of marketing for the XYZ Company returned from a seminar that had focused on participative management. Working in conjunction with the personnel department, he has decided to implement the concepts of "participative management" in the marketing department. Essentially, he sees participative management as integrating people in the work place by allowing them to take part in the decision-making process. In order to implement this management approach, a two-way (downward and upward) communication program is necessary to make employees aware of management goals and to make upper management aware of the participants' goals. This approach allows both management and its subordinates to agree on goal integration.

In view of this interplay between company and personal goals, the first major undertaking of participative management will be to involve marketing personnel at all levels in defining specific markets that will best utilize the company's resources so that some type of marketing decision model can be developed. As the vice president views it, it is a matter of selecting and balancing customer needs with the company products, along with considerations for employee needs. However, before this undertaking can be accomplished, the present effectiveness of the communications system within the marketing area must be determined.

The job of evaluating present communication effectiveness for marketing personnel has been delegated to the personnel vice president's assistant, who has decided to use a portion of the personnel management audit questionnaire, specifically the personnel overview section (see Figure 8-3). Inspection of the completed questions reveals several negative answers that need to be investigated further.

Although the first question, which centers on downward channels of communication, was answered with yes, the same cannot be said for the next question. An integral part of any participatory system is upward channels of communication that are not presently used to facilitate the accomplishment of marketing activities in an efficient and economical manner, not to mention marketing objectives. The third question places these marketing deficiencies in perspective. Negative answers (d and e) relating to matters affecting employee morale and employee needs indicate a cold and unfriendly atmosphere in the marketing environment.

The remaining negative answers also indicate an unfavorable marketing environment. Specifically, question 5 shows that marketing personnel are afraid to express their views and suggestions through formal communication channels. In like manner, question 7 states that they are not motivated sufficiently to take pride in their work. The negative answer to the last question is again indicative of the lack of concern for marketing personnel; communication channels are not employed to enhance their well-being.

Though not shown in this abbreviated case study, all subsections of the management audit questionnaire on communications for personnel and marketing were used. The reason for doing so was to determine the real nature of the communication problems before making final recommendations to the marketing vice president.

Recommendations to Improve Marketing Personnel Communications

Although the assistant to the personnel vice president was aware of some marketing communication difficulties, he was surprised by their magnitude. Uncovering these difficulties took him approximately three days. Since he had to report directly to his superior, the task proved to be difficult and required a high degree of tact and diplomacy. Nevertheless, he was able to develop final recommendations that were constructive and helpful in getting the marketing vice president's participation system off the ground.

Figure 8-3. XYZ Company evaluation of communications in marketing.

Personnel Part of Management Audit Questionnaire

	YES	NO	N.A.
I. PERSONNEL OVERVIEW			
E. Communication:			
1. Do the downward channels of communication facilitate the accomplishment of company objectives and activities in an efficient and economical manner?	X		
2. Do the upward channels of communication facilitate the accomplishment of company objectives and activities in an efficient and economical manner?		X	
3. Are there downward and upward channels of communication to provide for an efficient flow of information on:			
a. company programs and projects?	X		
b. company policies and directives?	X		
c. work methods and procedures?	X		
d. matters affecting employee morale?		X	
e. matters affecting employee needs?		X	
4. Are the general methods of communication effectively utilized:			
a. spoken or written words?	X		
b. numbers, including mathematics?	X		
c. pictures?	X		
d. actions?	X		
5. Are there organization policies to encourage employees to express their views and recommendations through formal communication channels?		X	
6. Are informal communication channels, i.e., the "grapevine," used to supplement the formal communication channels?	X		
7. Do communication channels provide the necessary information that motivates employees to take *pride* in their work?		X	
8. Do communication channels provide the necessary information that affects the employee's well-being, i.e., opportunity for advancement and seniority in a union?		X	

Questionnaire Comments (Negative Answers):
Question 2   Since the accent has been on the downward channels of communication, very few, if any, upward channels are utilized.

Question 3   (d and e) Accent is on the downward channels, with few or no upward channels, as is evidenced by the unfriendly atmosphere in the marketing department.

Question 5   The prevailing unfriendly atmosphere is not conducive to encouraging marketing personnel to express their views and recommendations.

Question 7   Under the prevailing conditions, marketing personnel do a fair job, which means that they do not, by and large, take pride in their work.

Question 8   Owing to the deficiency of upward communication channels, information necessary for the well-being of marketing employees is not always communicated.

The first recommendation centered on making effective use of the upward channels of communication. Although the marketing vice president makes great use of downward channels to keep his personnel informed on current marketing activities, he is remiss in employing upward channels, since his time to receive feedback from his personnel is necessarily limited. To overcome this difficulty, the sales manager, as well as the market research, advertising, and distribution managers, will act as ombudsmen to provide an avenue of complaints, grievances, and recommendations to the vice president in charge of marketing. In this manner, the benefits of active upward channels of communication will be received.

The second recommendation was that at least once a month marketing managers meet with their personnel. The purpose of these meetings is to let employees air their gripes as well as to listen to their ideas, opinions, and suggestions for improving marketing activities. Additionally, this recommendation included a provision for holding special periodic meetings to act on problems that arise unexpectedly and must be solved currently to keep marketing activities operating at a desired level. These meetings are to be initiated by marketing management so as to get marketing personnel involved in important decisions. Such regular and special meetings will provide greater information and knowledge about marketing problems, more approaches to and a better understanding of these problems, greater acceptance of and higher level of responsibility for decisions, and improved decision making.

To illustrate this last point, consider the opening statement made by the marketing vice president about getting personnel involved in defining specific markets for the best utilization of company resources. This goal can be accomplished by holding seminars that include everyone who can influence the marketing process—a first phase in developing and quantifying a marketing decision model. Such a marketing decision model needs the additive information that has been derived from man-to-supervisor contacts. When sufficient information flows up to the top, the model will contain all the important variables for reaching an optimum answer. When each group member knows the others' involvement with company goals, he or she can make a definite contribution to the model through the participatory process.

SUMMARY

The personnel function is not "an island unto itself" but rather an integral part of the functional areas found in an organization. This broad perspective provided the basis for the personnel part of the management audit questionnaire. The sections of the personnel questionnaire include the following: I. Personnel Overview, II. Manpower Planning, and III. Industrial Relations.

This division of personnel is helpful in pinpointing those areas that are experiencing difficulties. Overall, this important part of the questionnaire focuses on the "people problem," which can make or break any organization.

In addition to presenting the many questions for evaluating personnel management and the activities for which it is responsible, this chapter has applied the questionnaire to selected personnel problems. Personnel leadership and communication problems were pinpointed on the basis of the management audit questionnaire, and appropriate recommendations were made to improve personnel performance so as to achieve organizational objectives in a more efficient and economical manner.

V

MANAGEMENT AUDITING

of the
Work
Environment
and Information
System
Areas

9

Evaluating the
Work Environment
and
the Human Element

THE PRIOR CHAPTERS (3 through 8) have concentrated on the evaluation of
the major functional areas found in a typical industrial organization. Although a comprehensive management audit questionnaire by major business
functions is a necessity for a thorough analysis of an organization, it is not
complete without including the following sections:

> I. Work Structure
> II. Informal Structure
> III. Control of the Human Element

These sections form the subject matter for this chapter. They will be briefly
discussed below; the corresponding questionnaire is shown in Figure 9-1.

Because of the changing environmental factors affecting an organization,
the relevance of the work structure to the times must be evaluated. Is the
work structure responsive to the environmental changes taking place within
and outside the organization? Similarly, the informal structure should provide a means for satisfying more of the employee's needs on the job, in particular, those needs that cannot be satisfied through the formal work structure. Thus, in view of the current difficulties associated with the structure of
the work place, questions need to be directed toward highlighting "people
problems" as a starting point for resolving them or reducing them to tolera-
ble levels.

(text continues on page 202)

**Figure 9-1. Management Audit Questionnaire:
Work Environment and the Human Element.**

	YES	NO	N.A.

I. WORK STRUCTURE

    A. Work Environment Factors:

      General Considerations:

      1. Does the work environment structure allow recognition of the worker as an individual who has varying needs affecting his or her performance? ____ ____ ____

      2. Does the work environment structure allow recognition of the fact that the individual and his or her work within a group are both important in getting the job done (generally referred to as the *sociotechnical* approach)? ____ ____ ____

      3. Is there a *job enlargement* program in effect to overcome excessive specialization, that is, can the job content be enlarged to utilize more of the employee's abilities? ____ ____ ____

      4. Is there a *job enrichment* program in effect that permits vertical enhancement of the worker's tasks so as to allow an employee to participate in decisions concerning the tasks assigned? ____ ____ ____

      Sociotechnical Approach:

      1. Does the work environment allow the organization and development of teamwork under the direction and control of group leaders? ____ ____ ____

      2. Does the work environment permit the group to be self-regulated? ____ ____ ____

      3. Is it possible for members of the group to develop their skills and talents to the fullest? ____ ____ ____

      4. Is it possible for the members of the group to delegate authority for assignment of individual tasks? ____ ____ ____

      5. Do group members feel free to communicate with other members? ____ ____ ____

      6. Can group members learn every job performed by the group? ____ ____ ____

      7. Do group leaders work as equals with other group members? ____ ____ ____

      8. Does the work environment provide for a group monetary reward system? ____ ____ ____

	YES	NO	N.A.

Job Enlargement:

1. Does the job enlargement program entail informing and orienting employees concerning the significance of their work in relation to overall operations? ___ ___ ___

2. Is there rotation of workers among various jobs within a specialized work environment? ___ ___ ___

3. Does the work environment allow adding new duties to make the job more interesting and challenging? ___ ___ ___

4. Does the job enlargement program allow management the capability of improving acountability of workers? ___ ___ ___

5. Does the job enlargement program permit an increase in the quality of the product (through accountability)? ___ ___ ___

Job Enrichment:

1. Does the work environment allow adding new duties, such as reporting requirements, to make the job more interesting and challenging? ___ ___ ___

2. Does the job enrichment program allow the individuals within a work group to determine the work methods and sequence; for example, can a group assigned a general task divide the work according to its own choosing? ___ ___ ___

3. Does the job enrichment program allow shared responsibility among workers in setting their work pace and productive standards? ___ ___ ___

4. Does the job enrichment program permit worker participation in setting policies covering:
   a. work-break periods? ___ ___ ___
   b. overtime? ___ ___ ___
   c. layoffs? ___ ___ ___
   d. leaves of absence? ___ ___ ___
   e. corrective discipline (within a work group)? ___ ___ ___

5. Does the job enrichment program permit the work group to inspect its output? ___ ___ ___

6. Does the job enrichment program allow an ongoing employee training program for widened responsibilities and skills in handling a variety of jobs? ___ ___ ___

	YES	NO	N.A.

7. Does the job enrichment program allow management the capability of improving accountability of workers?

8. Does the job enrichment program encourage an increase in the quality of the product (through accountability)?

9. Does the job enrichment program consider individual preferences?

10. Does the job enrichment program allow a cost/benefit analysis?

B. Work Methods and Procedures:

General Considerations:

1. Are methods and procedures effective in processing the work?

2. Are methods and procedures flexible enough to bring about a cost reduction?

3. Have methods and procedures been established to ensure the completion of each and every specific task that must be performed in the work environment?

4. Are the methods and procedures being used as they were intended?

5. Are methods and procedures:
   a. set forth in writing?
   b. clear and understandable?

6. Are methods and procedures flexible enough to meet changing conditions?

7. Has sufficient consideration been given to internal control?

Office Environment:

1. Is the office properly laid out for efficient work flow?

2. Is the office laid out so as to realize maximum utilization of space?

3. Is maximum use made of present equipment?

4. Is the equipment best suited for the specific job(s)?

5. Is the equipment ideally located for optimum utilization by company employees?

6. Should certain methods and procedures be manual?

7. Have work units been identified and appropriate work standards developed?

	YES	NO	N.A.

8. Are current methods and procedures effective in accomplishing specific tasks? (That is, are there no operations that should be eliminated, simplified, combined, or improved by changing their sequence?)

9. Are there methods and procedures in effect to:
   a. recognize bottlenecks?
   b. eliminate them?

10. Have work simplification methods been employed to improve the paper flow?

11. Are inexperienced personnel capable of handling routine work?

12. Are exception items normally handled by experienced personnel?

13. Are there safeguards established against possible irregularities?

14. Are methods and procedures adequate to measure:
    a. quality of work?
    b. cost of work?
    c. productivity?

15. Do departmental reports allow for comparison with:
    a. predetermined objectives?
    b. budgeted figures?
    c. past periods?

16. Are company employees held responsible and accountable for carrying out their assigned tasks?

17. Is there an effective system of forms control?

18. Is the span of control for departmental supervisors adequate, that is, can supervisors adequately oversee their workers?

19. Are files reviewed periodically for transfer to storage?

Factory Environment:
1. Is the plant well laid out to provide an efficient and orderly process of:
   a. production?
   b. materials handling?
   c. materials storage?
   d. associated functions?

	YES	NO	N.A.
2. Is the plant well laid out for keeping movement of goods between machinery and equipment at a minimum?	___	___	___
3. Is maximum use being made of present machinery and equipment?	___	___	___
4. Are the machinery and equipment best suited for the specific job(s)?	___	___	___
5. Are there programs for machinery, equipment, methods, and processes to:			
a. improve manufacturing operations?	___	___	___
b. simplify manufacturing operations?	___	___	___
c. lower manufacturing costs?	___	___	___
d. compare actual to standard times and costs?	___	___	___
6. Is there a program to remedy the problem of excess capacity?	___	___	___
7. Is there a program to level out the production flow in order to keep overtime at a minimum?	___	___	___
8. Is there an effective wage incentive system to keep manufacturing costs at a minimum?	___	___	___
9. Are current work methods and procedures effective in accomplishing specific manufacturing tasks? (That is, are there no operations that should be eliminated, simplified, combined, or improved by changing their sequence?)	___	___	___
10. Are there effective work methods and procedures to:			
a. recognize bottlenecks?	___	___	___
b. eliminate them?	___	___	___
11. Have work simplification methods been employed to improve the manufacturing flow?	___	___	___
12. Are there safeguards against fire, explosion, and the like, that is, are good safety practices employed for worker protection?	___	___	___
13. Are there safeguards against theft, sabotage, and the like?	___	___	___
14. Are methods adequate to measure:			
a. the quality of work?	___	___	___
b. the cost of work?	___	___	___
c. productivity?	___	___	___

	YES	NO	N.A.

15. Do manufacturing work center reports allow for comparison with:
    a. predetermined objectives?
    b. budgeted figures?
    c. past periods?
16. Are factory foremen held responsible and accountable for carrying out their assigned tasks (in specific work centers)?
17. Is there a time and motion study program in effect?
18. Is the time and motion study program working effectively?
19. Is there an effective preventive maintenance program?
20. Does the preventive maintenance program keep downtime to a minimum?
21. Is the span of control for factory foremen proper, that is, can foremen adequately supervise their workers?

II. INFORMAL STRUCTURE

A. <u>Overview</u>:

1. Does the informal organization structure facilitate the accomplishment of work?
2. Does the informal structure alleviate deficiencies in the formal structure?
3. Does the informal structure contribute to lengthening the manager's effective span of control?
4. Does the informal structure compensate for the difficulty of applying certain formal organization principles; for example, do multiple superiors informally coordinate the control of the same subordinates for special situations?
5. Does management use the *grapevine* to increase organization effectiveness, that is, is it used to transmit accurate and useful information to employees?
6. Does the informal structure permit or encourage interpersonal contacts and friendships in the work environment?
7. Does the informal structure allow employees to satisfy their social needs on the job?

	YES	NO	N.A.
8. Does the informal structure stimulate management to be more sensitive to employees' needs?	___	___	___

B. Work Environment (Office or Factory):

	YES	NO	N.A.
1. Does the informal structure operate to further:			
a. company objectives?	___	___	___
b. individual needs?	___	___	___
2. Is the work environment (office or factory) structured, formally as well as informally, so that employees can use their talents to the fullest?	___	___	___
3. Is the work environment structured so that employees can cope with the problems of specialization—such as boredom, apathy, and general psychological fatigue—through the informal structure?	___	___	___
4. Does the work environment have a provision for evaluation leading to:			
a. self-renewal?	___	___	___
b. an improvement in human problems caused by specialization?	___	___	___
5. Is the work environment organized so that employees supplement and complement each other in:			
a. abilities?	___	___	___
b. activities?	___	___	___
6. Does the work environment allow employees to accomplish their tasks by:			
a. employing their own approaches to the job?	___	___	___
b. switching assignments and tasks among themselves?	___	___	___
7. Does the work environment allow for contacts that are not part of the formal structure to increase the efficiency of operations?	___	___	___
8. Are informal leaders utilized to supplement the formal organization structure to effect efficiency and economy in operations?	___	___	___
9. Are informal group leaders consulted before implementation of a major policy or change in methods and procedures?	___	___	___

	YES	NO	N.A.

10. Is the work environment relatively open so that new employees feel free to join groups based on common interests?

11. Are the informal groups allowed to develop structures and life styles that are separate from, but overlap, the prescribed work-centered relationships?

12. Does the informal structure promote status and give power to informal group leaders so as to satisfy more of their needs on the job?

13. Does the informal group tend to alleviate employees' insecurity about their jobs?

III. CONTROL OF THE HUMAN ELEMENT

A. Overview:

1. Does management exercise sufficient control over its employees to effect efficiency and economy in operations for accomplishing organization objectives?

2. Does management recognize that subordinate reaction to control is influenced by a number of factors operating within and outside the work environment?

3. Is an attempt made on the part of management to provide an open work atmosphere, especially where controls tend to be stringent?

4. Is corrective action undertaken from a positive viewpoint rather than a negative one?

5. Are management control systems designed with the human element in mind?

6. Does higher-level management support the "manager in the middle" (supervisory personnel) when controlling the human element at the lower levels?

7. Does management recognize the need for *variability* of controls—that is, the need to vary control systems according to the people being supervised, the caliber of supervision, and the work being performed?

YES   NO   N.A.

B. <u>Work Environment (Office or Factory):</u>

General Considerations:
1. Is control of the work environment predicated upon:
   a. the type of work being performed?   ___   ___   ___
   b. the type of employees on the job?   ___   ___   ___
2. Is there a tendency to "undercontrol" rather than to "overcontrol"?   ___   ___   ___
3. Does management attempt to provide a work environment that allows as many needs of the worker to be fulfilled on the job as is possible without impairing the accomplishment of organization goals?   ___   ___   ___
4. Does management anticipate employee reactions to controls so that appropriate changes can be made when reactions are deemed to be unfavorable?   ___   ___   ___
5. Does management allow for *changing* the distribution of control if the change simultaneously achieves individual satisfaction and organization effectiveness?   ___   ___   ___
6. Does management allow for *augmenting* the distribution of control if doing so simultaneously achieves individual satisfaction and organization effectiveness?   ___   ___   ___

Conflict Resolution:
1. Do the methods used for resolving conflict vary depending upon the situation?   ___   ___   ___
2. Does management make an attempt to uncover the underlying reasons for manager–subordinate conflicts?   ___   ___   ___
3. If employees are apathetic or indifferent to present and future conflict, does management develop a program to improve their attitudes toward the organization?   ___   ___   ___
4. Is the approach for resolving the conflict appropriate to the types of employees involved, i.e., positively or negatively motivated employees?   ___   ___   ___
5. Is there a set procedure for resolving manager–subordinate conflicts?   ___   ___   ___
6. Is the approach for resolving manager–subordinate conflicts such that there is

	YES	NO	N.A.

an open exchange of information and working out of the differences between the parties so that both can win (that is, is the *confrontation* approach employed)?

7. If the approach for resolving manager–subordinate conflict is not as stated in (6), is there at least an intermediate position of bargaining (that is, is the *compromising* approach employed)?

8. Is the approach used for conflict resolution conducive to reducing the potential for future conflict?

Performance Appraisal:

1. Does the organization have a performance appraisal program?

2. Does the performance appraisal program focus on:
   a. the individual's performance in accomplishing desired goals?
   b. the individual's performance in a certain position?

3. Does the performance appraisal program provide a means of observing subordinates for the purpose of identifying personnel for:
   a. merit increases?
   b. promotions?
   c. transfers?
   d. dismissals?

4. Does the performance appraisal program assist the manager in performing a more effective coaching job?

5. Does the performance appraisal program assist the manager in specifying the developmental needs of company personnel who have promotion potential?

6. Does the performance appraisal program motivate employees by providing feedback on their performance?

7. Does the performance appraisal program establish a research and reference base for personnel decisions?

8. Are the appropriate appraisal methods matched to desired performance goals?

Complementary to these two sections of the questionnaire is the one dealing with control of the human element. Specifically, the accent in this final section is on relating the human element to an open work environment, as opposed to the imposition of stringent controls. However, control of the work environment is conditioned by the type of employee (positively or negatively motivated) and the type of work being performed. Also included in this final section are questions on the resolution of manager-employee conflicts and on performance appraisals of employees.

COMMENTS ON THE WORK ENVIRONMENT AND HUMAN ELEMENT QUESTIONNAIRE

Work Structure

The advanced technology of today makes it necessary to focus on questions that are germane to work and its methods and procedures. Such questions are found in Section I of Figure 9-1, which evaluates the effectiveness of the work environment structure.

The benefits of technology and work systems are generally technical, while the drawbacks are predominantly human. Specialization, especially in the factory, often leads to personnel problems of boredom, apathy, meaninglessness, powerlessness, and insecurity. Attempts at simultaneous accomplishment of both specialization and humanization take the form of sociotechnical design of work teams, job enlargement, and job enrichment. (Job enlargement allows the individual to perform more tasks, whereas job enrichment allows the individual to participate in decisions concerning the tasks to be performed.) These areas form the basis for probing questions in subsection A, *Work Environment Factors*. If most questions are answered in the affirmative, the organization is doing a reasonably good job of optimizing human as well as technical values. On the other hand, too many negative answers mean there is need for humanizing the work environment.

Subsection B, *Work Methods and Procedures,* evaluates how effective methods and procedures are in carrying out the assigned tasks. Are the appropriate methods and procedures used to accomplish the desired results in terms of output or information for another functional area? How efficient are methods and procedures in accomplishing specific tasks? Basic questions of this type form the underlying structure of this subsection of the management audit questionnaire.

A subsection of Figure 9-1 will be evaluated for the XYZ Company to show how the questionnaire can be used to identify the technical and human problems within the work structure.

Informal Structure

Section II, which deals with the informal work structure, complements the preceding section on the formal work structure. The formal organization work structure specifies the appropriate set of duties for company personnel and their official interactions with others; by contrast, the informal organization structure develops naturally from the needs of people and the environment in which they find themselves. Inasmuch as people are social beings, they will engage in activities and interactions that are not an official part of the formal structure. Important major information relationships center on status, power, and politics. Counterparts in the formal structure, though not exactly equivalent, are responsibility, authority, and accountability.

In subsection A, general questions evaluate the capability of the informal work structure to enhance and complement the formal work structure. Affirmative answers to all questions indicate that management employs this structure to accomplish the desired objectives of the formalized structure. Within subsection B, questions focus more specifically on the quality of the work environment of the office or factory. Is much of the work performed in an open atmosphere? Do employees usually work in an informal manner? Negative answers indicate that the formal work structure may be too rigid and inhibiting for company employees. If so, it should be modified so that the informal structure can supplement it in order to achieve organization objectives more efficiently and economically.

Control of the Human Element

This part of the questionnaire (see section III of Figure 9-1) complements the preceding parts (found in this chapter and prior chapters) of the questionnaire. Since people are involved in the control system, it is only natural that the "people function" be evaluated as to its effectiveness.

In subsection A, general questions focus on how much importance management places on the human element when controlling operations. In effect, management should adapt the control system to the situation—the people, the supervision, and the work performed. Questions in subsection B become more detailed; the main concern is on the degree of control exercised over the individual. When operating conditions permit, organization personnel should be allowed as much latitude as possible in their work so as to enable them to satisfy more of their needs on the job. When this is not possible, there is always a problem of conflict between management and its subordinates. As indicated by the questions, these differences should be worked out. In the last section of the questionnaire, performance appraisal is evaluated.

Rather than explain this part of the management audit questionnaire further, a subsection will be applied to the XYZ Company.

APPLICATION OF MANAGEMENT AUDIT QUESTIONNAIRE TO THE COMPUTERIZED-ORDER-PROCESSING OFFICE ENVIRONMENT

Just a few days ago, the XYZ Company's vice president in charge of the computerized information system received complaints from his manager of data processing operations. The manager said that there has been a slow-down in processing incoming orders with the new on-line order processing procedures. Customer sales orders arrive by mail, telephone, and Teletype or are hand-carried by company sales personnel. When a check is attached, a memo is made on the order before forwarding it to the cash receipts section of the accounting department.

A CRT (cathode-ray tube) input/output (I/O) terminal which is connected to the computer system is used for order processing. Initially, the visual display terminal asks for customer identification. The operator enters the customer number unless the transaction is for a new customer, in which case the customer's name, address, and other information are entered. If an established customer's number is unknown, the name is entered and the system displays a list of "sound alike" customer names from which a selection is made. The computer system then flashes on the display screen successive requests for the entry of data pertaining to the order, and the operator enters these data. The questions relate to the customer order number, ship-to number, date of order, tax code, salesperson number, number of items ordered of each product, and catalog number. Also, the job control number is displayed. Questions about the order continue until the last item is entered. When all questions have been answered, the computer checks the customer's credit and either approves the order for filling or, if there is a credit problem, holds it up and automatically prints out a warning message on an I/O terminal in the credit section of the accounting department. Once the order has passed the credit check, additional computer processing takes place, such as accumulating finished goods for sales analyses and relieving finished-goods inventory.

Because of the slowdown in processing new orders, the vice president asked one of his senior system analysts to investigate the situation. The analyst employed the work structure section of the management audit questionnaire on methods and procedures for the office environment (orginally shown in Figure 9-1).

The completed questionnaire, shown in Figure 9-2, highlights strengths and weaknesses of ordering procedures. Although most answers indicate that

Figure 9-2. XYZ Company evaluation of computerized-order-processing office environment.

	YES	NO	N.A.
I. WORK STRUCTURE			
B. Work Methods and Procedures:			
Office Environment:			
1. Is the office properly laid out for efficient work flow?	X		
2. Is the office laid out so as to realize maximum utilization of space?	X		
3. Is maximum use being made of present equipment?		X	
4. Is the equipment best suited for specific job(s)?	X		
5. Is the equipment ideally located for optimum utilization by company employees?	X		
6. Should certain methods and procedures be manual?	X		
7. Have work units been identified and appropriate work standards developed?	X		
8. Are current methods and procedures effective in accomplishing specific tasks? (That is, are there no operations that should be eliminated, simplified, combined, or improved by changing their sequence?)		X	
9. Are there methods and procedures in effect to:			
a. recognize bottlenecks?		X	
b. eliminate them?		X	
10. Have work simplification methods been employed to improve the paper flow?		X	
11. Are inexperienced personnel capable of handling routine work?	X		
12. Are exception items normally handled by experienced personnel?		X	
13. Are there safeguards established against possible irregularities?	X		
14. Are methods and procedures adequate to measure:			
a. quality of work?	X		
b. cost of work?	X		
c. productivity?	X		
15. Do departmental reports allow for comparison with:			
a. predetermined objectives?	X		
b. budgeted figures?	X		
c. past periods?	X		

	YES	NO	N.A.
16. Are company employees held responsible and accountable for carrying out their assigned tasks?	X		
17. Is there an effective system of forms control?	X		
18. Is the span of control for departmental supervisors adequate, that is, can supervisors adequately oversee their workers?	X		
19. Are files reviewed periodically for transfer to storage?	X		

Questionnaire Comments (Negative Answers):

Question 3   Maximum use of present equipment, i.e., visual (CRT) display terminals, is not being made, because inexperienced operators must stop their work and ask experienced operators or supervisory personnel how to handle complex orders. Consequently, several display terminals are not being utilized to their fullest capacity.

Question 8   Current order processing procedures are not effective, because inexperienced terminal operators are processing complex orders, which they are not always capable of handling.

Question 9   Current methods and procedures are not in effect to recognize order processing bottlenecks, as evidenced by the present situation.

Question 10   Work simplification methods, such as the separation of routine orders from complex orders, have not been employed in the past to speed up the paper flow.

Question 12   Unfortunately, exception items are handled by inexperienced personnel. As a result, more errors than normal are going through the order processing system.

---

the office environment is compatible with on-line computerized ordering procedures, several questions have been answered negatively. The comment on question 3 indicates that visual (CRT) display terminals are not used to the fullest possible extent in the new work environment. Similarly, current methods and procedures (see question 8) are not effective in processing the incoming orders. The negative answer to question 9 shows that no methods are in effect to recognize order processing bottlenecks and remedy them. In addition, work simplification methods have not been employed (see question 10). The answers to questions 11 and 12 reveal another inefficient situation: inexperienced personnel are handling both routine and complex orders.

Recommendations to Improve the Computerized-Order-Processing Office Environment

After a thorough analysis of the facts as revealed by the questionnaire, the system analyst made some straightforward recommendations to the vice president in charge of the information system. Since all orders must be entered on-line through a visual display terminal, the logical approach is to segregate routine orders from complex orders before they are given to personnel for on-line processing. This segregation can be accomplished upon receipt, with each section of the company receiving sales orders forwarding two separate groups of orders. Orders that contain a few items to be shipped from one warehouse are to be processed by inexperienced personnel. Those orders that contain ship-to instructions and items to be shipped from several warehouses are to be handled by experienced personnel. This new approach allows both inexperienced and experienced personnel to excel at what they do best.

Although the foregoing recommendation rectifies the basic problem, another recommendation is needed to deal with recognizing and eliminating office bottlenecks. One solution is to set performance standards that are based on output for various levels of experience. Each operator's output should be compared daily to what is expected. Essentially, those individuals who fail to produce at a satisfactory level will undergo additional training or be transferred to another job.

APPLICATION OF MANAGEMENT AUDIT QUESTIONNAIRE TO SALES WORK ENVIRONMENT

Just last week at a management seminar, the executive vice president of the XYZ Company met a marketing vice president of a firm comparable in size to XYZ, but in a totally different industry. They discussed a method that facilitates management's ability to evaluate sales performance. The executive vice president was impressed with what he heard; he planned to implement such a sales performance system.

Upon his return, he called in the marketing vice president and the controller to set the wheels in motion. He directed both men to work together and devise a control system that would facilitate evaluation of sales personnel performance. After an extensive investigation by all three individuals, it was decided to realign sales territories so as to make them more equal in terms of sales potential. In this manner, performance comparisons could be made on a more equitable basis. In addition, a report was designed that required each salesperson to recap his or her daily work. These reports were to be used by the accounting department to compare the productivity of salespersons with established standards.

Once the details of the new sales performance program were formalized, the salespersons were advised that some kind of control was forthcoming next week. When the actual procedures, which included the realignment of sales territories, were announced, the older salespersons voiced strong objections. Several of them had large territories that they had serviced for over twenty years. They had established extremely good relationships with key customers, and as a result they enjoyed high commissions with a minimum of effort.

Because of the unfavorable reaction, the vice president in charge of marketing was caught in the middle between the objections of his salespersons and the demands of the controller and the executive vice president, who maintained that realignment of territories was necessary for any control. After some effort by the marketing vice president to explain the situation to the salespersons, the control system was put into effect despite the warnings from the salespersons, who predicted a decline in sales if customer relationships were disturbed.

As the salespersons had predicted, sales began to decline, which was partly the result of a deliberate slowdown by the salespersons. Established customers complained, and a few went elsewhere for their goods. When two of the company's top salespersons threatened to seek employment with competitors, the executive vice president decided to reevaluate his position.

Before returning to the past method of aligning sales territories, the executive vice president directed his assistant to review the situation and be as objective as possible in his evaluation before making final recommendations. To assist in his review, the assistant decided to use the performance appraisal subsection of the management audit questionnaire (see section III of Figure 9-1). This completed section along with explanations of the negative answers is presented in Figure 9-3.

Inspection of the completed questionnaire reveals only one negative answer (question 6). The realignment of sales territories to make them more equal in terms of sales potential fails to motivate salespersons, since it means lower commissions for many of the company's salespersons. In addition, this reshuffling means that all salespersons must establish new contacts, which may be difficult to do in certain situations. Thus, the new sales appraisal program motivates sales personnel in a *negative,* not a positive, way.

To ensure that the problem had been evaluated properly, the staff assistant completed the entire *Control of the Human Element* section of the management audit questionnaire (see Figure 9-1, section III). On the basis of this review, the essential facts for making final recommendations were delineated.

Figure 9-3. XYZ Company evaluation of sales work environment.

Work Environment and Human Element Part of
Management Audit Questionnaire

	YES	NO	N.A.

III. CONTROL OF THE HUMAN ELEMENT

  B. Work Environment (Office or Factory):

    Performance Appraisal:

    1. Does the organization have a performance appraisal program?   **X**   ___   ___

    2. Does the performance appraisal program focus on:
      a. the individual's performance in accomplishing desired goals?   **X**   ___   ___
      b. the individual's performance in a certain position?   **X**   ___   ___

    3. Does the performance appraisal program provide a means of observing subordinates for the purpose of identifying personnel for:
      a. merit increases?   ___   ___   **X**
      b. promotions?   ___   ___   **X**
      c. transfers?   ___   ___   **X**
      d. dismissals?   ___   ___   **X**

    4. Does the performance appraisal program assist the manager in performing a more effective coaching job?   **X**   ___   ___

    5. Does the performance appraisal program help the manager in specifying the developmental needs of company personnel who have promotion potential?   **X**   ___   ___

    6. Does the performance appraisal program motivate employees by providing feedback on their performance?   ___   **X**   ___

    7. Does the performance appraisal program establish a research and reference base for personnel decisions?   ___   ___   **X**

    8. Are the appropriate appraisal methods matched to desired performance goals?   **X**   ___   ___

Questionnaire Comments (Negative Answers):

Question 1   Because of the adverse effect of this sales performance program, this yes answer needs to be explained. Although a program has recently been implemented for evaluating performance of salespersons within specified sales territories, the firm is experiencing declining sales caused *directly* by this new performance appraisal method.

Question 6   The recently installed sales performance program fails to motivate salespersons, since their commissions have been cut in many cases.

Recommendations to Improve the Sales Work Environment

To assist in developing recommendations to the executive vice president, the staff assistant mulled over the facts in his mind. His first thought was, "How could this unfortunate occurrence have been avoided?" Initially, there was the question of whether or not control was necessary, since sales had been rising for some time and the company had prospered without the sales performance program. Actually, nothing had been gained by indiscriminately establishing controls. Attempts to "tighten the screws in areas where the screws did not need to be tightened" caused dysfunctional behavior among the company's salespersons. Furthermore, salespersons devised a full set of informal rules for filling out the daily sales reports so that one salesperson did not "show up" the others. Hence, the control method was essentially useless.

In view of these observations, the staff assistant recommended that management personnel involved in setting up the sales performance program also be involved in establishing a new sales control program. However, this time management will let the salespersons help design the controls and set the standards. This participation by the salespersons will be instrumental not only in securing their cooperation, but also in creating a sense of obligation to exceed the standards. The salespersons will also find the reports useful in revealing weaknesses in their sales coverage. Thus, the recommendation of getting the salespersons involved in the sales performance appraisal program will solve the basic problem as well as the symptoms related to it.

In this situation, participation serves to benefit the company and its salespersons. The company gains the increased sales and profits; the salespersons realize higher commissions. The outcome is similar to the "confrontation" approach to resolving conflicts, in which an open exchange of information and working out of the differences results in *both* parties winning.

SUMMARY

In this chapter, the main focus has been on the work environment and the human element as an essential part of the management audit questionnaire. The major sections for this part of the questionnaire (after presentation of all functional areas in the prior chapters) are as follows: I. Work Structure, II. Informal Structure, and III. Control of the Human Element.

This breakdown serves to highlight those areas that may not be functioning according to predetermined organizational objectives, caused in part or whole by ineffective management.

Also highlighted in the chapter has been the application of this part of the management audit questionnaire to selected problems of the XYZ Company, namely, the company's computerized office environment and the sales work environment. With the aid of the questionnaire, managerial and operational deficiencies were detected and eliminated so as to meet organizational objectives as originally intended.

10

Evaluating the Information System

A MANAGEMENT AUDIT QUESTIONNAIRE for evaluating an information system (IS) provides a basic framework for determining the degree of managerial and operational control over the computer system. Extenuating circumstances such as natural disasters may relate to a computer system, creating the need for questions and investigations not covered in this part of the questionnaire. The individual reviewing the system must exercise his or her judgment in this regard. Whether or not additional questions are appended, the questionnaire is designed to determine if at least a minimum degree of control is being maintained in an information system.

The major sections of the information system questionnaire (see Figure 10-1) are:

> I. Computer Department Controls
> II. Input, Programmed, and Output Controls
> III. Interactive and Security Controls

It should be noted that additional sections could have been added, for example, hardware controls. As indicated, however, the foregoing is comprehensive enough to detect most managerial and operational deficiencies of an information system.

The presentation of the information system management audit questionnaire is followed by two sample applications for the XYZ Company. They are oriented toward computer department and security controls.

(text continues on page 222)

Figure 10-1. Management Audit Questionnaire: Information System.

	YES	NO	N.A.

I. COMPUTER DEPARTMENT CONTROLS

  A. General Considerations:

    1. Is the computer department under the direction of a qualified manager? ____ ____ ____

    2. Are the computer department's long-range plans adequate for meeting the company's objectives? ____ ____ ____

    3. Has management made ample computer plans for handling the company's future growth? ____ ____ ____

    4. Does management employ current hardware and software in its computer operations? ____ ____ ____

    5. Does information system management exert the necessary leadership to get the funds it needs to support effective computer operations? ____ ____ ____

    6. Does information system management motivate its personnel to do an effective job in providing the desired level of data processing services? ____ ____ ____

    7. Does information system management exercise the necessary control over its operations so that fraud, theft, and inaccuracies of DP methods and procedures can be detected? ____ ____ ____

    8. Does information system management employ the appropriate security measures to minimize fraud, theft, and inaccuracies? ____ ____ ____

  B. Organization:

    1. Is the computer department operating as a separate unit without direct control over the company's assets? ____ ____ ____

    2. Is the computer department centrally located for best use? ____ ____ ____

    3. Are the following personnel groups, located within the computer department, organizationally and physically separate from one another:

      a. punched-card personnel? ____ ____ ____

      b. computer operators? ____ ____ ____

      c. systems analysts and programmers? ____ ____ ____

	YES	NO	N.A.

    d. computer supervisory personnel and auditors?

    e. programs and records (tapes and disks) librarians?

  4. Are all computer programmers and operators frequently transferred to different machines and programs?

  5. Are system and programming personnel forbidden to operate the computer for regular data processing runs?

  6. Is there an internal auditor to check on the operations of the computer department?

C. Methods and Procedures:

  1. Are there established written procedures for all DP activities outside the computer department?

  2. Is there standardization for system flowcharts and program flowcharts?

  3. Are programming techniques standardized within the computer department?

  4. Are there established procedures for program testing?

  5. Have all standardized procedures been compiled in a computer manual?

  6. Is the computer manual current?

  7. Are there established procedures for making program changes?

  8. Are all program changes immediately documented, including the reason for the change?

II. a. INPUT CONTROLS

  A. General Considerations:

    1. Does information system management require that input controls be made an integral part of its information system?

    2. Are newer input controls instituted by information system management to reflect changing conditions of input methods and procedures, such as from a batch processing mode to an interactive mode?

YES   NO   N.A.

3. Does information system management require that input controls start
with the first input processing
methods and procedures?   ___   ___   ___

4. Are input controls reviewed periodically by an independent third party,
i.e., DP consultants or auditors, to
make sure that they serve the pur-
pose for which they were intended?   ___   ___   ___

B. Verification Methods:

1. Are all important data fields verified
for punched card or paper tape to
ensure accuracy of input informa-
tion?   ___   ___   ___

2. If input medium is not punched card
or paper tape, is the degree of accu-
racy adequate?   ___   ___   ___

3. If conversion equipment and data
transmission equipment are used to
convert or transmit data (input), is
adequate verification being per-
formed?   ___   ___   ___

C. Input Control Totals:

1. Are batch control totals established
before sending data to the compu-
ter?   ___   ___   ___

2. If no batch control totals are utilized,
is there some other means of establishing input control, such as
hash totals and record count totals?   ___   ___   ___

3. Are all input documents prenum-
bered and accounted for by an independent count so that all transac-
tions received are processed?   ___   ___   ___

4. Is responsibility fixed for errors on
input documents so that corrective
action can be taken?   ___   ___   ___

5. Are input-error corrective methods
properly controlled to ensure that
actual correction and re-entry into
the system is accomplished?   ___   ___   ___

D. External Labels:

1. Do external labels contain sufficient
information for their effective use?   ___   ___   ___

YES   NO   N.A.

2. Is there an adequate procedure for documenting magnetic tape and disk pack labels in the computer area? ⎯ ⎯ ⎯

II. b. PROGRAMMED CONTROLS

A. General Considerations:

1. Are programmed controls required by information system management? ⎯ ⎯ ⎯
2. Are programmed controls fully understood and implemented by the programming staff? ⎯ ⎯ ⎯
3. Are programmed controls reviewed periodically by an independent third party, i.e., consultants or auditors, to make sure that they serve the purpose for which they were intended? ⎯ ⎯ ⎯

B. Validation Checks and Tests:

1. Is sequence checking used to verify the sorted input data? ⎯ ⎯ ⎯
2. Are data fields checked for correct type of data—alpha, numeric, zero, blank, and special characters? ⎯ ⎯ ⎯
3. Do code numbers, such as account number and inventory number, make use of the self-checking digit technique? ⎯ ⎯ ⎯
4. Are limit or reasonableness tests utilized where needed? ⎯ ⎯ ⎯
5. Do programs test input data for valid codes, and are printouts or halts provided when invalid codes are detected? ⎯ ⎯ ⎯
6. Do programs make use of check points when processing must be restarted after its initial start? ⎯ ⎯ ⎯
7. Do computer loading routines include tests that verify the successful loading of a computer program? ⎯ ⎯ ⎯

C. Computer Control Totals:

1. Do computer programs provide continuance of input control (i.e., batch totals, hash totals, and record count totals)? ⎯ ⎯ ⎯

	YES	NO	N.A.

2. Are the following control techniques utilized in the various computer programs:
   a. balancing totals?
   b. cross-footing balance check?
   c. zero balancing?
   d. proof figures?
3. Are the completeness and accuracy of the various files checked during processing?
4. Are changes in program rate tables and other data initiated in writing and under the control of authorized personnel?
5. Are program changes retained for audit?
6. Is there an on-line procedure for the detection and skipping of bad portions of magnetic tape?
7. Are all halts, excluding end of job, recorded and retained for audit?

D. Internal Labels:

   1. Do header labels have adequate information—program identification, reel number, date created, and date of obsolescence?
   2. Do trailer labels contain appropriate information—block count, record count, data totals, and end-of-label?
   3. Do programs test for header and trailer labels each time a new tape or disk is accessed or the end of the tape reel or disk is sensed?

E. Error Routines:

   1. Is there an adequate program procedure for identifying, correcting, and reprocessing errors?
   2. Are all instructions to computer operators set forth in writing for effective processing control as well as handling of error conditions?
   3. Are console operators cautioned not to accept oral instructions and not to contact programmers directly when errors are found?

YES   NO   N.A.

II. c. OUTPUT CONTROLS

A. General Considerations:

1. Are output controls specified by information system management? ___ ___ ___

2. Are newer output controls instituted by information system management to reflect changing conditions of output methods and procedures, such as from a batch processing mode to an interactive processing mode? ___ ___ ___

3. Does information system management require that output controls be made an integral part of its information system? ___ ___ ___

4. Are output controls reviewed periodically by an independent third party, i.e., DP consultants or auditors, to make sure that they serve the purpose for which they were intended? ___ ___ ___

B. Output Control Totals:

1. Can output data be compared with predetermined totals (batch totals, hash totals, or record count totals)? ___ ___ ___

2. Are provisions made within the information system to reconstruct files in the event that the current files are damaged or destroyed? ___ ___ ___

3. Are corresponding transactions being stored in reprocessible form for emergency operations? ___ ___ ___

C. Control by Exception:

1. Are all exception items immediately and properly investigated? ___ ___ ___

2. Is corrective action undertaken for all exception items? ___ ___ ___

3. Is there a periodic verification of master file balances, such as inventory and payroll, to correct erroneous data and check for irregularities? ___ ___ ___

D. Control over Operator Intervention:

1. Are procedures in force that prevent access of operators and other unauthorized personnel to programs for perpetuating fraud? ___ ___ ___

	YES	NO	N.A.

2. Are typewriter console printouts controlled and reviewed by designated personnel, e.g., internal auditors? ___ ___ ___

3. Is effective control exercised over the operator's adherence to processing procedures? ___ ___ ___

4. Is there a periodic surprise audit of the computer room to check for program irregularities by computer operators? ___ ___ ___

III. a. INTERACTIVE CONTROLS

A. General Considerations:

1. Are interactive controls required by information system management? ___ ___ ___

2. Are interactive controls fully understood and implemented by the system staff? ___ ___ ___

3. Are interactive controls reviewed periodically by an independent third party, i.e., consultants or auditors, to make sure that they serve the purpose for which they were intended? ___ ___ ___

B. On-Line Processing Controls:

1. When input/output terminals are used for data transmission, are the following control techniques used:

a. message identification (identifies each message received by the computer)? ___ ___ ___

b. message transmission control (assures that all messages transmitted are actually received)? ___ ___ ___

c. message parity check (verifies the accuracy of the message sent)? ___ ___ ___

2. Is there adequate control over terminals in case it is necessary to retransmit the data? ___ ___ ___

3. Is access to confidential information properly controlled? ___ ___ ___

C. Data Protection Controls:

1. Are supervisory protection programs in effect to handle the problem of concurrent updating and the resultant loss of data? ___ ___ ___

YES   NO   N.A.

2. Are lockwords or passwords and authority lists utilized for data security?   ——   ——   ——

3. Is there a monitoring routine that counts the number of unsuccessful attempts (say 3 or 4) to enter the system and initiates a procedure to handle the difficulty?   ——   ——   ——

D. Diagnostic Controls:

1. Are diagnostic programs, in conjunction with a supervisory program, used to detect and isolate error conditions for proper corrective action?   ——   ——   ——

2. Are there sufficient on-line programmed controls to handle the following conditions:

a. restart the program in question?   ——   ——   ——
b. reexecute the faulty instruction?   ——   ——   ——
c. switch control to an error routine?   ——   ——   ——
d. initiate a switchover to another on-line system?   ——   ——   ——
e. shut down part of the system?   ——   ——   ——
f. halt the system?   ——   ——   ——

3. Are checkpoint records developed as processing occurs so as to facilitate a restart?   ——   ——   ——

4. Are there manual emergency procedures to handle a halt in the computer system?   ——   ——   ——

III. b. SECURITY CONTROLS

A. General Considerations:

1. Are security controls required by information system management?   ——   ——   ——

2. Are security controls fully understood and implemented by the systems staff?   ——   ——   ——

3. Are security controls reviewed periodically by an independent third party, i.e., consultants or auditors, to make sure that they serve the purpose for which they were intended?   ——   ——   ——

B. Specific Considerations:

1. Are master files stored under conditions that provide reasonable protection against damage or destruction?   ——   ——   ——

	YES	NO	N.A.
2. Is there a schedule of all current computer programs which includes an identification number, date, and description?	___	___	___
3. Are all computer programs properly documented?	___	___	___
4. Are computer programs and supporting materials maintained in the records library and issued to persons with written authorization?	___	___	___
5. Are adequate daily equipment logs being properly maintained?	___	___	___
6. Are adequate daily equipment logs being reviewed for irregularities?	___	___	___
7. Is entrance to the computer room limited to computer operators and authorized personnel?	___	___	___
8. Are there procedures for preventing premature reuse of magnetic tapes and disks?	___	___	___
9. Are there adequate controls to prevent premature erasures of data from magnetic tapes and disks?	___	___	___
10. Is there an established policy for the retirement of magnetic tape reels with excessive read or write errors?	___	___	___
11. Is the computer system serviced by qualified service engineers on a regular basis?	___	___	___
12. Are manufacturers' temperature and humidity requirements maintained?	___	___	___

COMMENTS ON THE INFORMATION SYSTEM QUESTIONNAIRE

Computer Department Controls

Section I of the questionnaire centers on general considerations plus the data processing organization and its control methods and procedures. The purpose of this section is to determine the department's efficiency or lack thereof. Lack of effective control here indicates potential problems.

In evaluating the organization of the computer department, relationship of data processing personnel to one another is scrutinized for possible collusion. Likewise, those who operate computer programs they have written are investigated thoroughly. Effective control dictates that computer activities be separate and distinct from one another.

Methods and procedures within the computer department are evaluated basically in light of standardization and documentation. Questions are asked concerning the established procedures in handling systems and operational activities. Of great importance is the degree of documentation practiced by the department. Too often, this important aspect is ignored by systems personnel in favor of more challenging DP tasks. Poor control over DP methods and procedures is a reflection on the department's management.

Input, Programmed, and Output Controls

Section II contains questions for evaluating input, programmed, and output controls within the information system. Within each area, initial focus is on general management considerations. Because the remaining areas are somewhat technical, a brief description of each area is presented below. The questions for input, programmed, and output controls, other than those pertaining to general considerations, are oriented toward the operations aspects of an information system.

Input Controls

Control of computer input data is defined as the set of procedural controls necessary to handle data outside the computer area. Extreme care must be taken in handling these data, since input data are the most probable source of errors in the entire information system. If errors are created anywhere between the origination point and input into the computer equipment, they will be carried forward throughout the entire system. In order to keep errors to a minimum, the following procedural controls over input data are available for an information system: verification methods, input control totals, and external labels.

Verification methods. Some degree of input verification is absolutely necessary for consistently reliable results. The extent and methods employed are best determined by comparing the level of undetected errors against the cost of verification. Only in this manner can verification devices assure the accuracy and validity of input data. Verification methods include *key verification, visual verification, self-checking numbers,* and *tabular listings.* Although these verification devices are not associated electronically with a computer system, they are just as important as the computer itself. Their function is to check the accuracy of raw data that are converted into a computer-acceptable language.

Input control totals. Control totals that aid in determining the accuracy of input data are generally obtained from adding machine tapes or from totals established in originating departments. Careful system design can provide a high level of accuracy with very little additional effort and expense. Control totals (batch totals, hash totals, and record count totals) are usually taken on batches or groups of source documents. Batching with a control total is the most common method for ensuring input accuracy.

External labels. External labels, another form of input controls, are visible labels attached to a magnetic tape or disk. Certain identifying information can be written on the tape or disk label. Information that may be a part of the label includes: name of run, type of information, density, reel number, number of reels in the file, frequency of use, date created, drive number, earliest date it might be reused, record count, and the individual's name responsible for the tape or disk. The purpose of external labels is to make sure that the correct input file is processed by the computer operator and that data are not destroyed prematurely.

Programmed Controls

A high degree of programmed computer controls is always advisable, since undetected errors can have serious and far-reaching consequences. Programmed control steps should be included as a part of the machine's internally stored instructions. The extent of controls depends upon the relationship between increased costs in programming and machine time on the one hand and the resulting increase in accuracy on the other. In the case of on-line programmed controls, the programming ability of the data processing section, the requirements of the particular run, and the capabilities of the equipment must also be taken into account.

Since most computer applications are slowed down by the speeds of input/output units, the central processor has generally more than sufficient time to perform the necessary control checks. Therefore, the number of programmed controls is dependent upon the amount of program memory available. If sufficient space is available for program instructions, the programmer should include as many controls as necessary. They can be classified as follows: validation checks and tests, computer control totals, internal labels, and error routines.

Validation checks and tests. Validation comprises a series of checks and tests that can be applied to verify input, file, and calculated data during the computer processing run. Such validation includes sequence checks, character mode tests, self-checking digit tests, limit checks, code validity tests, blank transmission tests, alteration tests, and check points. The inclusion of all or part of these processing controls is contingent upon the program itself.

Computer control totals. Computer control totals are a continuation of the input control techniques described previously: *batch controls, hash totals,* and *record count totals.* Errors uncovered by any one of these control techniques during computer processing may be handled as the program requires. The entire group of data may be rejected immediately, or it may be allowed to pass through for current processing. In the latter case, it is customary to store the error conditions and report them externally as a printout. There are additional computer totaling techniques that provide procedural control during processing. These are balancing controls, cross-footing balance checks, zero balancing, and proof figures.

Internal labels. The internal label of a magnetic disk or tape is an extension of the external data label. Certain identifying information can be written on the disk or tape. It is under the control of the computer program in the form of a lead record. Before actual computer processing begins, the program reads the lead record to ascertain that the correct magnetic disk pack or magnetic tape has been mounted on the proper input equipment. If the computer stops and indicates an incorrect input disk or tape, one of two possible error conditions could be present: either the wrong input device was utilized, or the external label does not correspond to the internal label.

Error routines. There are several ways of handling error routines. The most common method is to treat the error routine as an integral part of the internally stored program. If errors are detected as a result of the validation checks, processing tests, and computer control totals, the program can instruct the computer to store the data, punch a data card, print the data, or initialize some other method for bringing the error condition to light for external handling and correction. Under no circumstances would the processing run be halted. This is in contrast to error routines which halt the computer for major problems. Examples of problems that would require halting the computer are: magnetic tape file is out of sequence, input cards are out of sequence, magnetic bits of data are being lost, or incorrect magnetic disk is being addressed.

Output Controls

The role of the computer as a center of control is accentuated even more when output controls are present. While input controls ensure that all data are processed, output controls assure that results are reliable. This promotes operational efficiency within the computer area with regard to programs, processed data files, and machine operations. Output controls also ensure that no unauthorized alterations have been made to data while they were under the control of the computer. Output controls can be classified as follows: output control totals, control by exception, and control over operator intervention.

Output control totals. The major categories for output control totals, set forth under input and programmed controls above, are essential for control of output data. The most basic of all output controls is the comparison of *batch control totals* with figures that preceded the computer processing stage. If the batch totals are in agreement with the pre-computational figures, input data most probably have been processed accurately. (However, it is conceivable that two or more internal errors canceled each other, so batch totals do not represent a perfect control.) In the absence of batch control totals for certain programs, the comparison of *output hash totals* or *record count totals* to predetermined figures will substantiate the validity of the data. No matter what output approach is used for control totals, the job of checking their accuracy belongs to the internal auditor or a designated employee.

Periodically, computer processing should be audited by tracing individual transactions from the originating department through the computer and its related files to output control totals. Such tests assure that data are being processed accurately and in accordance with the company's methods and procedures.

Control by exception. The individuals responsible for output control should also be responsible for investigating exceptions. These exceptions could include recurring errors, excessive inventories, sales to customers who have exceeded their credit limit, higher prices for raw materials purchases, or deviations from established sales prices. If computer programs are properly designed for processing routine items and highlighting exceptions, management can focus on exceptional data for more effective decision making. To assist managers, most advanced computer systems make great use of this control-by-exception technique.

Control over operator intervention. Controlling operator intervention is a problem common to all computer facilities. Generally, programmed controls do not prevent the console operator from interrupting the data being processed and manually introducing information through the computer console. Even if the internally stored program does possess a routine for printing out all information introduced, the operator is still able to suppress the printout on the console typewriter. However, if the typewriter is discovered turned off, the operator would immediately be suspect. In those systems where changes can be effected without a hard-copy record, the need for supervising the computer's operation increases. However, research has indicated that unauthorized console interventions are kept to a minimum where there is rotation of computer operators and, in particular, where output controls are exercised over all computer printouts.

Interactive and Security Controls

Like the previous sections, the last major section of the information system management audit questionnaire initially focuses on general management considerations. Specific questions on interactive and security controls follow. Due to the technical nature of the subject matter, interactive and security controls are explained in more detail below.

Interactive Controls

Computer system controls are applicable to all information systems, whether they are batch processing or interactive processing systems. However, additional controls are necessary to ensure an adequate two-way flow of information in an interactive environment. In fact, such systems create many new problems not found in batch processing systems. For example, how can confidential data be made accessable only to authorized personnel? What happens to data in the system when the computer is down for repairs? How can accuracy be assured with interactive processing?

Generally, controls will be dictated by such factors as the requirements of the system, the equipment itself, and security specifications. The areas discussed below are not all-inclusive, but they are representative of the control requirements found in a typical interactive system. They include on-line processing controls, data protection controls, and diagnostic controls.

On-line processing controls. On-line processing controls are necessary because messages from and to the input/output terminal devices can be lost or garbled. It is possible that the terminal will go out of order during transmission or receipt of data. To guard against working with incorrect data under these conditions, the system should provide program routines for checking on messages. These routines are: message identification, message transmission control, and message parity check.

Data protection controls. Data protection controls provide answers to many interactive questions. Questions include: What happens when two separate transactions are trying to update concurrently the same record? What assurance is there that program segments read into the computer's memory will not be accidentally read in over data currently being processed? What procedures are followed to prevent unauthorized access to the system?

Diagnostic controls. One of the difficulties with any interactive system is a malfunction of the equipment or a programming error that occurs during the system's operations. The best method is to keep the system operating, provided the trouble can be circumvented. This approach can be accomplished if diagnostic programs are used to detect and isolate error conditions for proper corrective action. However, once the problem has been determined, it is up to the supervisory program to make the necessary adjustments. It can restart the program in question, reexecute the faulty instruction, switch control to an error routine, initiate a switchover to another system, shut down part of the system, or halt the system. The first three are used to overcome software problems, while the latter three are necessary to control hardware malfunctions.

Security Controls

Computer system controls and hardware controls are essential for a successful information system. The same can be said for security controls. Basically, these are controls over contingencies not adequately encompassed by other controls. They offer a means of preserving essential data when reprocessing becomes necessary, and protecting against computer errors that might otherwise not be detected.

For security controls to be effective, they must be standardized for day-to-day operations. When security procedures are not followed precisely, variable control follows, resulting in operational difficulties and inconsistent corrective action. Most computer installations have the following security controls: program control, equipment log, records control, tape rings, and preventive maintenance.

Information system controls and their relationship to a computer are summarized in diagrammatic form in Figure 10-2.

APPLICATION OF MANAGEMENT AUDIT QUESTIONNAIRE TO THE COMPUTER DEPARTMENT

Some time ago, the vice president of marketing for the XYZ Company made several derogatory remarks to the vice president of information systems concerning the long order-processing time required for a customer order. To be more specific, the time required to process an order at the company's field warehouse is seven days. In contrast, the marketing executive stated, two of the company's competitors were processing orders in less than half the time.

Since this type of problem could have a sizable impact on the company's sales in the near future, the vice president of information systems immediately engaged the services of outside computer consultants to study the problem and make recommendations that could be implemented on a crash basis. To assist in their analysis, the information system part of the management audit questionnaire, as set forth in the chapter, was completed. However, since not all areas are directly applicable, only the subsection on computer department controls, shown in Figure 10-3, was included.

These positive answers to questions 1 and 3 indicate that the information system area is under capable management and that the current batch processing mode can handle the company's future data processing growth. However, question 2 discloses the fact that long-range department plans are not adequate to meet company objectives. Specifically, the computer department's present method of processing orders requires twice as much time as that of its two competitors. Hence, the company's objective of providing fast customer service on incoming orders is not met when compared to com-

Figure 10-2. Relationship of information system controls to a computer.

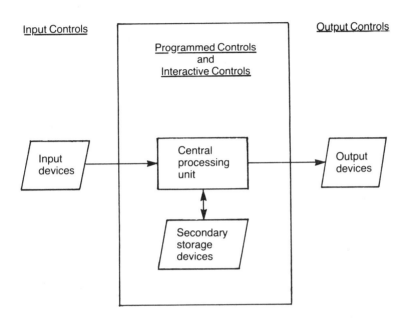

Security Controls

Input Controls

Output Controls

Programmed Controls
and
Interactive Controls

Input
devices

Central
processing
unit

Output
devices

Secondary
storage
devices

petition. In a similar manner, the answer to question 4 indicates that information system management may not be progressive enough in acquiring the latest in hardware and software for maintaining a high level of customer service. The long order-processing time has been caused by the utilization of batch processing equipment and procedures.

The remaining questions have been answered in the affirmative. Information system management exerts the necessary leadership to get the funds needed for updating computer operations, motivates its personnel, has sufficient control over its operations for detecting fraud and inaccuracies, and employs appropriate security controls. Overall, the vice president in charge of information systems has taken a traditional approach to order processing in the past; that is, he has relied heavily on a batch processing mode rather than newer developments in this area.

Recommendations to Improve the Computer Department

Utilizing the foregoing information, the outside consultants made one major recommendation. Fundamentally, it involves undertaking a thorough feasibility study to determine the possibility of upgrading the present batch-

Figure 10-3. XYZ Company evaluation of computer department controls.

	YES	NO	N.A.

I. COMPUTER DEPARTMENT CONTROLS

A. General Considerations:

	YES	NO	N.A.
1. Is the computer department under the direction of a qualified manager?	X		
2. Are the computer department's long-range plans adequate for meeting the company's objectives?		X	
3. Has management made ample computer plans for handling the company's future growth?	X		
4. Does management employ current hardware and software in its computer operations?		X	
5. Does information system management exert the necessary leadership to get the funds it needs to support effective computer operations?	X		
6. Does information system management motivate its personnel to do an effective job in providing the desired level of data processing services?	X		
7. Does information system management exercise the necessary control over its operations so that fraud, theft, and inaccuracies of DP methods and procedures can be detected?	X		
8. Does information system management employ the appropriate security measures to minimize fraud, theft, and inaccuracies?	X		

Questionnaire Comments (Negative Answers):

Question 2 Due to the shortened service time of processing customer orders by its two competitors, the computer department's long-range plans are not in tune with the company's objectives of providing fast and dependable customer service on orders.

Question 4 Currently, the company utilizes only batch processing equipment and procedures in processing customer orders, even though newer interactive equipment and procedures have been available for several years.

oriented processing system for incoming orders and replacing it with a more advanced system. Specifically, the consultants contemplate the use of "intelligent" terminals that are capable of interacting with a processor for on-line processing. In essence, each evening data are forwarded from the company's warehouses to corporate headquarters. The next morning processed information is transmitted back for order pulling. In this manner, the internal time to process a customer order totals three days—one day to process the order using interactive equipment from and to the company warehouses, one day for scheduling the order and pulling the order for shipment, and one day for loading and shipping to the customer.

Although the outside consultants are confident that the above data processing approach to order processing will work, they have recommended that a more systematic and efficient approach be used. The proposed feasibility study approach includes the following steps:

- *Introductory investigation*—establishes the study group and defines the scope of the order processing study.
- *System analysis*—includes an analysis of the present order processing system, including all of its problems and exceptions.
- *Exploratory survey report to top management*—centers on developing a report that recommends one order processing system.
- *System design*—stresses the design of new order processing equipment, data files, and outputs along with appropriate methods and procedures.
- *Equipment selection*—concludes the feasibility study with the selection of appropriate interactive processing equipment for on-line processing of incoming customer orders.

Thus, an appropriate recommendation has been set forth to overcome the present excessive order processing time.

APPLICATION OF MANAGEMENT AUDIT QUESTIONNAIRE TO SECURITY CONTROLS

The executive vice president of the XYZ Company just finished reading an article on computer fraud. The article mentioned the case of the Equity Funding Corporation of America, which has revealed some gaping holes in computer security and control methods. Officials in Equity used the corporation's computer to create false insurance policies and to inflate the apparent financial status of their company. The fall of Equity Funding, together with a number of related scandals in other organizations, has made it clear to the executive vice president that there is a real threat to the XYZ Company from inside the computer center itself. Thus, he reasoned that systems personnel, with their highly specialized knowledge and skills and their easy access to operating hardware and programs, can rob or defraud the company in such a way that their depradations can go undetected for months and possibly for an indefinite period of time.

In view of the possibility of computer theft, fraud, and the like in the information system area, he called in the outside auditors. While meeting with them, he stressed the need for going beyond the normal audit and spending a week during the interim review work on the computer department alone. Although this extended the scope of the regular audit, the executive vice president felt that the money spent investigating this area in great detail would be of benefit to the company, particularly since the company manufactures and sells high-demand consumer products that can be easily sold on the outside.

The outside auditors brought in data processing experts from their staff. Being accustomed to reviewing computer systems in depth, they utilized the information system management audit questionnaire set forth in the chapter (see Figure 10-1).

After a thorough review of the computer system, the outside DP experts concluded that the computer department was generally well managed and that input, programmed input, and interactive controls were operating as intended, except for control over operator intervention and a few small items. However, the same could not be said for security controls, which exhibited major deficiencies (see Figure 10-4).

A review of this subsection reveals several deficiencies of computer operations. As the negative answer to question 4 indicates, computer programs and supporting materials maintained in the records library are accessible to all company personnel, thereby allowing anyone to get hold of a program and alter it. Similarly, the computer department is deficient in its method of handling time on the computer. As the answers to questions 5 and 6 indicate, even though a daily equipment log is maintained, nobody checks to make sure that all computer time is accounted for. Thus, there are many cases where available computer time is unexplained. Finally, the negative answer to question 7 indicates that some unauthorized personnel have been seen in the computer room.

Recommendations to Improve Security Controls

Overall, the main thrust of the negative answers in Figure 10-4 is that managerial control over computer security leaves a lot to be desired. This was the essential content of the verbal presentation that the outside computer experts made to the executive vice president. As one of them said, "Things are

Figure 10-4. XYZ Company evaluation of security controls in the computer department.

	YES	NO	N.A.
III. b. SECURITY CONTROLS			
B. Specific Considerations:			
1. Are master files stored under conditions that provide reasonable protection against damage or destruction?	X		
2. Is there a schedule of all current programs that includes an identification number, date, and description?	X		
3. Are all computer programs properly documented?	X		
4. Are computer programs and supporting materials maintained in the records library and issued to persons with written authorization?		X	
5. Are adequate daily equipment logs being properly maintained?		X	
6. Are adequate daily equipment logs being reviewed for irregularities?		X	
7. Is entrance to the computer room limited to computer operators and authorized personnel?		X	
8. Are there procedures for preventing premature reuse of magnetic tapes and disks?	X		
9. Are there adequate controls to prevent premature erasures of data from magnetic tapes and disks?	X		
10. Is there an established policy for the retirement of magnetic tape reels with excessive read or write errors?	X		
11. Is the computer system serviced by qualified service engineers on a regular basis?	X		
12. Are manufacturers' temperature and humidity requirements maintained?	X		

Questionnaire Comments (Negative Answers):

Question 4   Computer programs and supporting materials maintained in the records library are available to computer personnel without written authorization.

Question 5   Although daily logs of computer time are being maintained, they are incomplete, since computer operators and programmers testing programs fail to log in and out at all times.

Question 6   Inasmuch as there are gaps in the equipment logs of computer time, they are never investigated.

Question 7   Entrance to the computer room is generally limited to computer operators and authorized personnel. On occasion, however, unauthorized personnel have been seen in the computer room.

---

loose as a goose.'' To rectify this problem, their first recommendation revolved around improved managerial controls over computer processing time as well as the programs themselves. The current situation is such that a programmer could obtain a program (magnetic tape), alter it using the computer, and return it without anybody noticing. In a few words, this is a very bad situation, since it allows computer personnel the capability of stealing the company blind by altering payroll, inventory, and similar programs.

An important part of this first recommendation is that a computer records librarian be hired to monitor and maintain the computer records library and issue computer programs and supporting materials to authorized personnel only. In this manner, there will be a complete record of what programs were used by whom and at what time. If there is any question regarding the altering of computer programs and related materials, the individual can be identified.

A second recommendation centers on the proper maintenance of daily equipment logs. The outside DP experts recommended that the internal auditor have the responsibility of reviewing this log time sheet for irregularities. As a typical example, a computer program that has been operational for a long time should be tested by the auditor, since it lends itself to unauthorized alteration.

Third, the outside computer group recommended that the computer operations manager enforce the policy that only authorized personnel are allowed in the computer room. In this manner, needless problems can be avoided, such as someone dropping a magnetic tape file without reporting it. In essence, the computer room is a storehouse of information that can be costly to replace if someone accidentally or willfully destroys computer file information.

Other recommendations were presented, based upon minor problems found in the prior sections of the management audit questionnaire. However, the foregoing represented the major problems and recommendations to overcome them.

SUMMARY

A comprehensive review of any computer system can be obtained by utilizing the information system management audit questionnaire set forth in this chapter. Specifically, the questionnaire was divided into the following sections: I. Computer Department Controls, II. Input, Programmed, and Output Controls, and III. Interactive and Security Controls.

Not only does this questionnaire highlight those computer functions that may not be operating in an efficient manner, but it also brings to light those managerial areas that may be deficient in an information system.

As with prior chapters, two sample applications of the information system part of the management audit questionnaire have utilized selected subsections of the questionnaire. These subsections have provided a beginning point for making final recommendations to overcome information system deficiencies.

Bibliography

Auerbach, Norman E. "ABCs of Audit Committees." *Financial Executive,* October 1976.

Baker, John K., and Robert H. Schaeffer. "Making Staff Consulting More Effective." *Harvard Business Review,* January–February 1969.

Buckley, John W. "Management Services and Management Audits by Professional Accountants." *California Management Review,* Fall 1966.

Burch, J. B., Jr., and J. L. Sardinas, Jr. *Computer Control and Audit: A Total Systems Approach.* New York: Wiley & Sons, 1978. (Reference for Chapter 10 of this text)

Burton, John C. "Management Auditing." *The Journal of Accountancy,* May 1968.

Buskirk, Richard H. *Handbook of Managerial Tactics.* Boston: CBI Publishing Company, 1976.

Campbell, J. P., M. D. Dunnette, E. E. Lawler, III, and E. E. Weick, Jr. *Managerial Behavior, Performance, and Effectiveness.* New York: McGraw-Hill, 1970.

Carmichael, Douglas R. "Some Hard Questions on Management Audits." *The Journal of Accountancy,* February 1970.

Clarke, Robert W. "Extension of the CPA's Attest Function in Corporate Annual Reports." *Accounting Review,* October 1968.

Davidson, Frank. *Management Consultants.* London: Nelson & Sons, 1972.

Davis, Gordon B. *Auditing and EDP.* New York: American Institute of CPA's, 1968.

De Vos, Henry. *Management Services Handbook.* New York: AICPA's, 1964.

Drucker, Peter F. "A New Scorecard for Management." *The Wall Street Journal,* September 24, 1976.

Dykeman, Francis C. *The Contributions of Management Auditing in Financial Reporting.* Englewood Cliffs, N.J.: Prentice-Hall, 1970.

Fertakis, John P., and Bruce R. Budge. "Management Services by the Controller's Department." *Managerial Planning,* May–June 1974.

Forchheimer, Otto L. "Accountability for Functional Executives." *S.A.M. Advanced Management Journal,* April 1972.

Fuchs, Jerome H. *Making the Most of Management Consulting Services.* New York: AMACOM, 1975.

Greenbaum, Howard H. "The Audit of Organization Communication." *Academy of Management Journal,* Volume 17, Number 4, 1974.

Greenwood, William T. *A Management Audit System,* rev. ed. Carbondale, Ill.: School of Business, Southern Illinois University, 1967.

———. *Business Policy: A Management Audit Approach.* New York: Macmillan, 1967.

Guck, E. "The Psychology of Management Audits." *Management Accounting,* September 1974.

Hayek, Anthony. "Management Audits and the Outside Consultant." *Industry* (London, England), March 1950.

Jordan, Henry H., Jr. "A Checklist for Production and Inventory Controls." *Management Review,* August 1970.

Kelly, William F. *Management Through Systems and Procedures.* New York: Wiley & Sons, 1969.

Langenderfer, Harold Z., and Jack C. Robertson. "A Theoretical Structure for Independent Audits of Management." *Accounting Review,* October 1969.

Lazzaro, Victor (ed.). *Systems and Procedures.* Englewood Cliffs, N.J.: Prentice-Hall, 1959. (Chapter 5, "The Management Audit")

Leonard, William P. *The Management Audit.* Englewood Cliffs, N.J.: Prentice-Hall, 1962.

Lewis, Ralph F. "What Should Audit Committees Do?" *Harvard Business Review,* May–June 1978.

Lindberg, Roy A. "Operations Auditing," *Management Review,* December 1969.

Lindberg, Roy A., and Theodore Cohn. *Operations Auditing.* New York: AMACOM, 1972.

Lippitt, Gordon, and Ronald Lippitt. *Consulting Process in Action.* La Jolla, California: University Associates, 1978.

Lovdal, Michael L. "Making the Audit Committee Work." *Harvard Business Review,* March–April 1977.

Lovdal, Michael L., Raymond A. Bauer, and Nancy H. Treverton. "Public Responsibility Committee of the Board." *Harvard Business Review,* May–June 1977.

Management Services Questionnaire. Prepared by Committtee on Management Services, California Society of CPA's, 1964.

Martindell, Jackson. *The Scientific Appraisal of Management.* New York: Harper & Row, 1962.

———. *Manual of Excellent Managements.* New York: American Institute of Management, 1957.

McFarlan, F. Warren. "Management Audit of the EDP Department." *Harvard Business Review,* May–June 1973.

McIntyre, Gordon. "Auditing for Management Control." *Management Review,* November 1975.

Mintzberg, H. *The Nature of Managerial Work.* New York: Harper & Row, 1973.

Morse, John J., and Francis R. Wagner. "Measuring the Process of Managerial Effectiveness." *Academy of Management Journal,* Volume 21, No. 1, 1978.

Porter, L. W., and E. E. Lawler, III. *Managerial Attitudes and Performance.* Homewood, Ill.: Richard D. Irwin, 1968.

Schaffer, Robert H. "Demand Better Results—And Get Them." *Harvard Business Review,* November–December 1974.

Scott, George M., and H. Bart. "The Internal Audit—A Tool for Management Control." *Financial Executive,* March 1978.

Secoy, Thomas G. "A CPA's Opinion on Management Performance." *The Journal of Accountancy,* July 1971.

Smith, Charles H., and Roy A. Lanier. "The Audit of Management: Report on a Field Study." *Management Accounting,* June 1970.

Smith, Lee. "The Boardroom Is Becoming a Different Scene." *Fortune,* May 8, 1978.

Snellgrave, Olin C. "The Management Audit: Organizational Guidance System." *Management Review,* March 1972.

Spett, Milton C. "Standards for Evaluating Data Processing Management." *Datamation,* December 1969.

Staats, Elmer B. "The Multipurpose Audit." *Management Review,* June 1971.

Thierauf, Robert J. *Data Processing for Business and Management.* New York: Wiley & Sons, 1973. (Chapter 16 for data processing system controls)

Thierauf, Robert J., Robert C. Klekamp, and Daniel W. Geeding. *Management Principles and Practices: A Contingency and Questionnaire Approach.* Santa Barbara, Calif.: Wiley/Hamilton, 1977. (Chapters 2, 8, 12, 16, and 20 for a management audit on a functional basis)

Wendell, Paul J. (ed.) *Modern Accounting and Auditing Checklists.* Boston: Warren Gorham & Lamont, 1977.

White, H. C. "A Leadership Audit." *Management Accounting,* August 1973.

Witte, Arthur E. "Management Auditing: The Present State of the Art." *The Journal of Accountancy,* August 1967.

Wooton, Leland M., and Jim L. Tarter. "The Productivity Audit: A Key Tool for Executives." *MSU Business Topics,* Spring 1976.